SURVIVAL ENGLISH

ENGLISH THROUGH CONVERSATIONS

BOOK 2

Lee Mosteller

Michele Haight

San Diego Community College District

Illustrated by Jesse Gonzales

PRENTICE HALL REGENTS, Englewood Cliffs, NJ 07632

Library of Congress Cataloging-in-Publication Data

Mosteller, Lee.
  Survival English: English through conversations, book 2 / Lee
Mosteller, Michele Haight.
    p. cm.
  ISBN 0-13-879199-6
    1. English language—Textbooks for foreign speakers. 2. English
language—Conversation and phrase books. I. Haight, Michele.
II. Title.
PE1128.M7434 1988   87-25841
428.3´4—dc19   CIP

Editorial/production supervision and
  interior design: Patricia V. Amoroso
Cover design: Lundgren Graphics, Ltd.
Manufacturing buyers: Margaret Rizzi and Peter Havens

 © 1988 by Prentice-Hall, Inc.
A Division of Simon & Schuster
Englewood Cliffs, New Jersey 07632

Printed in the United States of America

10 9 8 7 6 5 4 3

ISBN 0-13-879199-6 01

PRENTICE-HALL INTERNATIONAL (UK) LIMITED, *London*
PRENTICE-HALL OF AUSTRALIA PTY. LIMITED, *Sydney*
PRENTICE-HALL CANADA INC., *Toronto*
PRENTICE-HALL HISPANOAMERICANA, S.A., *Mexico*
PRENTICE-HALL OF INDIA PRIVATE LIMITED, *New Delhi*
PRENTICE-HALL OF JAPAN, INC., *Tokyo*
SIMON & SCHUSTER ASIA PTE. LTD., *Singapore*
EDITORA PRENTICE-HALL DO BRASIL, LTDA., *Rio de Janeiro*

*This is dedicated to our ESL students
with our respect and friendship.*

CONTENTS

PREFACE

This book is designed for the ESL student who has a limited oral vocabulary, a limited reading ability, and some use of the alphabet. The student is probably not functionally literate or fluent in English. *Survival English: English Through Conversations, Book 1* provides a helpful prerequisite to this book. Students at this level bring to the classroom common experiences from the community and the motivation to learn the survival skills necessary to function in daily life.

This book is organized to develop listening, speaking, reading, and writing skills, in that order. It provides competency-based dialogues in four content areas appropriate for the low-literate adult learner. The dialogues provide listening and speaking practice incorporated with familiar and necessary living skills. They are followed by charts, reading passages, sequence stories, and exercises to reinforce and develop the competencies introduced in the dialogues. The writing activities are patterned to provide the learner with much practice at a low level and based on language patterns the learner can orally produce.

ABOUT THE SURVIVAL ENGLISH SERIES

By Lee Mosteller and Bobbi Paul:

Book 1
Book 1A (contains chapters 1-5 of Book 1)
Book 1B (contains chapters 6-10 of Book 1)
Instructor's Manual for Book 1

By Lee Mosteller and Michele Haight:

Book 2
Book 2A (contains chapters 1-4 of Book 2)
Book 2B (contains chapters 5-9 of Book 2)
Instructor's Manual for Book 2

1

SCHOOL

SCHOOL 1

Name _____

A. I want to learn   to speak English.
　　　　　　　　　　　to drive.
　　　　　　　　　　　to sew.
　　　　　　　　　　　to weld.
　　　　　　　　　　　to type.
　　　　　　　　　　　citizenship.

B. Go to school.

A. Where?

B. Adult school.

A. When?

B. I'm not sure. Let's look in the schedule.

Adult School Schedule

Class	Day	Time	Location	Teacher
ESL 1	M, W, F	8:30–11:30	High School	May
ESL 2	M, W, F	8:30–11:30	High School	White
ESL 3	T, Th	9:00–12:00	High School	May
ESL 4	T, Th	9:00–12:00	High School	White
Driving	F	1:00–3:00	Church	North
Typing	M, W	5:30–8:30	High School	Hart
Sewing	Th	6:00–9:00	Junior High	Johnson
Citizenship	T	6:00–9:00	Junior High	Smith

1. What time is the ESL 3 class?
2. When is the ESL 3 class?
3. Where is the ESL 3 class?
4. Who teaches the ESL 3 class?

SCHOOL 2

Teacher's name _____

A. Teacher, this is my friend _____ .

$\boxed{\begin{matrix} \text{He} \\ \text{She} \end{matrix}}$ is from _____ .

B. Welcome to school. It's nice to meet you.

A. $\boxed{\begin{matrix} \text{He} \\ \text{She} \end{matrix}}$ is a new student.

$\boxed{\begin{matrix} \text{He} \\ \text{She} \end{matrix}}$ wants to register for school.

4

SCHOOL 3

A. Welcome to school. Here's your registration card. Please fill it out.

B. I forgot my social security number.

A. That's O.K. Bring it tomorrow.

B. O.K. I will.

ADULT SCHOOL REGISTRATION CARD

Name _____

           Last   First

Address _____

         Number   Street

      _____

      City   State   Zip code

Telephone _____

Soc. Sec. No. _____

Date of birth _____

In case of emergency call _____

      Phone _____

Signature _____

Date _____

---

1. My name is _____ .

2. My address is _____

   _____ .

3. My telephone number is _____ .

4. My social security number is _____ .

5. My teacher's name is _____ .

6. I'm from _____ .

7. I speak _____ .

8. My friend's name is _____ .

9. _____ address is _____

   _____ .

10. _____ telephone number is _____ .

11. _____ is from _____ .

12. _____ speaks _____ .

SCHOOL 4

I'm from _____.

A. Remember to come to school tomorrow.
B. I will.
A. Don't forget to bring a pencil.
B. I won't.

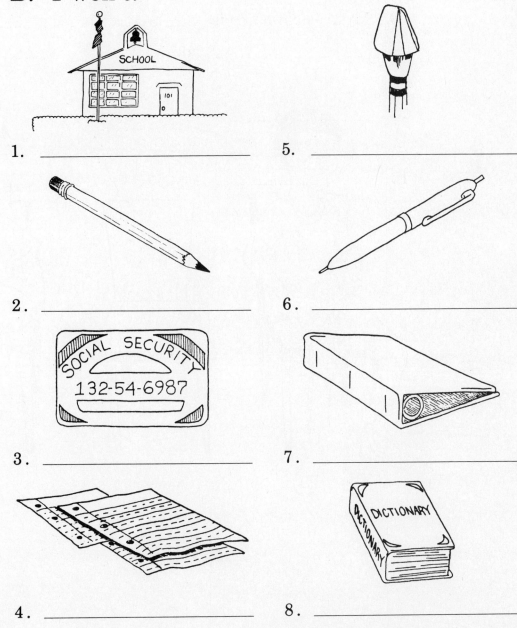

1. _____

5. _____

2. _____

6. _____

3. _____

7. _____

4. _____

8. _____

SCHOOL 5

I speak _____.

    A. Is anyone sitting here?
    B. I'm not sure. Ask him.
    A. Is anyone sitting here?
    C. No. Sit down.

SCHOOL 6

Telephone _____

A. Oh no!

B. What's the matter?

A. I can't find my pencil.
I think I forgot it.

B. Here. Borrow mine. I have an extra one.

1. I can't find my _____.

2. I think I forgot _____.

3. I have _____ _____.

4. I can't find my _____.

5. I think I forgot _____.

6. I have _____ _____ .

I You We They	think	I you we they	forgot.
He She	thinks	he she	

1. I can't find my pens.

    I _____ _____ _____ them.

2. He can't find his dictionary.

    He _____ _____ _____ it.

3. They can't find their papers.

    They _____ _____ _____ them.

4. She can't find her social security card.

    She _____ _____ _____ it.

5. We can't find our pencils.

    We _____ _____ _____ them.

6. He can't find his eraser.

    He _____ _____ _____ it.

7. She can't find her registration card.

    She _____ _____ _____ it.

8. They can't find their notebooks.

    They _____ _____ _____ them.

SCHOOL 7

I want to learn _____.

A. Do you have little children?

B. Yes, I do.

A. Who is taking care of them now?

B. My
| husband |
| wife |
| babysitter |
| _____ |

A. Do they go to
| preschool |
| nursery school |
| day care |
?

B. No, they don't. They're on the waiting list for preschool.

SCHOOL 8

Soc. Sec. No. _____

A. Are your children in school?

B. Yes, they are.

A. Where do they go?

B. My son goes to elementary school.
He's in fourth grade.
My daughter goes to high school.
She's in tenth grade.

Name	Age	School	Grade

AGE	GRADE	SCHOOL
2 3 4		nursery
5 6 7 8 9 10 11	kindergarten 1 2 3 4 5 6	elementary
12 13 14	7 8 9	junior high
15 16 17	10 11 12	senior high
18 19 20 . . .		adult job training vocational

1. La is eight years old.

    He's in _____ grade.

    He goes to _____ school.

2. Xanh is sixteen years old.

    He's in _____ grade.

    He goes to _____ school.

3. Xay is four years old.

    She's in _____ school.

4. Tom is fourteen years old.

    He's in _____ grade.

    He goes to _____ school.

5. Phai is twenty-six years old.

    She goes to _____ school.

6. Anna is five years old.

    She's in _____ .

    She goes to _____ school.

7. Joe is fifty-three years old.

    He goes to _____ _____ .

8. I'm _____ years old.

    I go to _____ _____ .

SCHOOL 9

School _____

A. _____ , I'm not coming to school tomorrow.

B. What's the matter?

A. I'm busy. I have to talk to my son's teacher.

B. That's fine. Thank you for telling me.

1. I _____ not coming. I _____ to talk to my son's teacher.

2. They _____ not coming. They _____ _____ talk to their son's teacher.

3. She _____ not coming. She _____ _____ _____ to her son's teacher.

4. He _____ not coming. He _____ _____ _____ _____ his son's teacher.

Age _____

A. My name is _____ .

   My son is _____ .

B. Good morning. It's nice to meet you. I want to talk to you about his report card.

A. How is he doing?

B. He's doing very well. He works hard.

GRADES

E	A	Excellent
	B	Very good
S	C	O.K.
	D	Needs help
U	F	Needs lots of help

Address _____

_____

A. Good morning, Mrs. Johnson.

B. Hello, Mr. North. How is my daughter doing in school?

A. Her behavior is excellent. Her spelling is not very good.

B. Can you give her some extra homework in spelling?

A. Yes, I can. She needs to work more on her spelling.

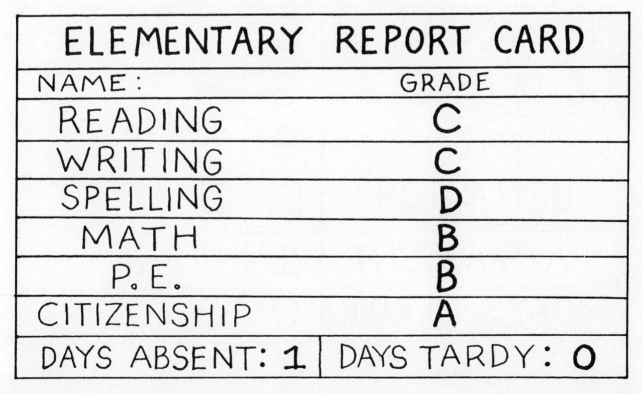

ELEMENTARY REPORT CARD	
NAME:	GRADE
READING	C
WRITING	C
SPELLING	D
MATH	B
P. E.	B
CITIZENSHIP	A
DAYS ABSENT: 1	DAYS TARDY: 0

REPORT CARD

STUDENT'S NAME: ANN DIN				GRADE: 7
SUBJECT	FIRST	SECOND	THIRD	FINAL
READING	C	B	A	B
ENGLISH	B	C+	B	B
SPELLING	A	A-	B+	A
MATHEMATICS	A	A	A	A
SCIENCE	C	B	A	B
PHYSICAL EDUCATION	S	S	S	S
MUSIC	S	S	S	S
ART	S	S	S	S
BEHAVIOR	E	E	E	E
DAYS ABSENT	1	O	2	3
DAYS TARDY	O	3	1	4

REPORT CARD

STUDENT'S NAME: ANN DIN   GRADE: 7

SUBJECT	FIRST	SECOND	THIRD	FINAL
READING	C	B	A	B
ENGLISH	B	C+	B	B
SPELLING	A	A-	B+	A
MATHEMATICS	A	A	A	A
SCIENCE	C	B	A	B
PHYSICAL EDUCATION	S	S	S	S
MUSIC	S	S	S	S
ART	S	S	S	S
BEHAVIOR	E	E	E	E
DAYS ABSENT	1	0	2	3
DAYS TARDY	0	3	1	4

1. How many days was Ann late?

    _____

2. How many days was Ann absent?

    _____

3. What is her final grade in English?

    _____

4. What is her final grade in math?

    _____

5. Did her science grade go up or down?

    _____

6. Did her spelling grade go up or down?

    _____

7. What is her final grade in music?

    _____

8. What is her final grade in reading?

    _____

9. How is her behavior?

    _____

SCHOOL 12

I go to _____ school.

A. School office.

B. This is _____ . My son can't come to school today. He's sick.

A. What's his name?

B. His name is _____ .

A. What grade is he in?

B. _____ grade.

A. O.K. Thank you for calling.

1. My daughter can't come to school today.

   _____'s sick.

2. What's _____ name?

3. _____ name is Anna.

4. What grade is _____ in?

5. _____'s in second grade.

Every letter has five important parts:

1. the date
2. who it is to
3. what you want to say
4. the good-bye or thank-you
5. who it is from

February 28, 1987

Dear Teacher,

    Tom was sick. Please excuse him from school.

        Thank you,

        Mrs. Day

---

1. What's the date? _____

2. Who is it to? _____

3. What's the matter? _____

_____

4. Is there a good-bye or thank-you? _____

5. Who is it from? _____

Dear _____

_____

_____

_____

_____

_____

_____

_____

_____

CIRCLE ONE

1.	I wrote the date.	yes	no
2.	I wrote someone's name.	yes	no
3.	I wrote about something.	yes	no
4.	I wrote thanks or good-bye.	yes	no
5.	I signed my name.	yes	no

April 20

Dear Parents,

The second grade is going on a field trip to the <u>city zoo</u> on <u>Monday, April 28</u> by bus. Please fill out this form and return it to school.

My son/daughter _____
(student's name)

has my permission to go to the _____
(place)

on _____ by bus.
(date)

_____
parent's signature

_____
date

1. Who is this letter to?

   _____

2. Who is the letter from?

   _____

3. What is the letter about?

   _____

4. What's the date of the letter?

   _____

brings
is
talk

is
shaking
feels

| are | shake | brings | is | talk |

Joe _____ home a letter from school. The

letter _____ from his teacher. His teacher

wants to talk to his parents. She wants to have a conference.

The parents _____ hands with the teacher.

They _____ about Joe. His report card

_____ very good. Joe _____

happy and his parents _____ proud.

1. What did Joe bring home from school?
2. Who was the letter from?
3. Where did Joe's parents go?
4. Why was Joe happy?
5. How was his report card?

FROM: TEACHER

TO: PARENTS
NOVEMBER 12, 1987

1. I want to learn to speak _____ .

2. I want to register for _____ .

3. I remember my _____ and _____ .

4. I go to _____ school.

5. La is eight years old. He goes to _____ school.

6. La is a very good student. He has many A's on his _____ _____ .

7. There are five important parts in a _____ .

ELEMENTARY REPORT CARD	
NAME :	GRADE
READING	C
WRITING	C
SPELLING	D
MATH	B
P.E.	B
CITIZENSHIP	A
DAYS ABSENT: 1	DAYS TARDY: 0

2

CLOTHING

CLOTHING 1

Signature _____

A. _____ had a new baby.
B. Let's buy her a present.
A. That's a good idea.
B. Does she need baby blankets?
A. Yes, I think she does.

1. _____

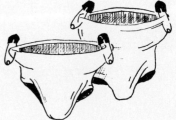

2. _____

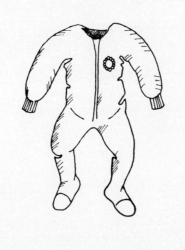

3. _____

4. _____

CLOTHING 2

Date _____

A. How much of this do you need?

B. Three yards.

A. O.K. It's $2.98 a yard. Do you need a zipper or thread?

B. No, thanks. Just the fabric.

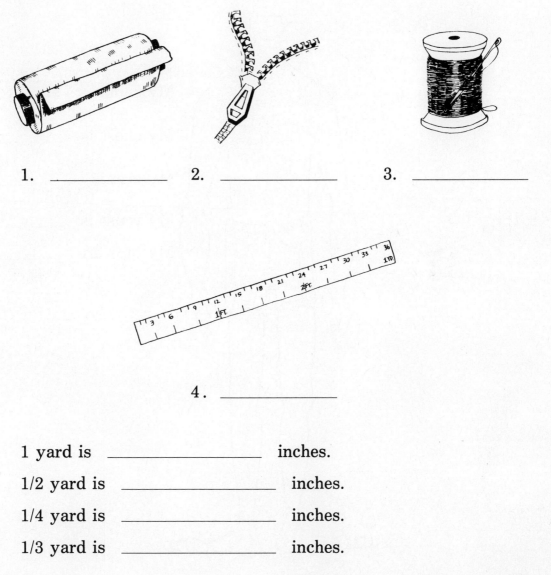

1. _____   2. _____   3. _____

4. _____

1 yard is _____ inches.

1/2 yard is _____ inches.

1/4 yard is _____ inches.

1/3 yard is _____ inches.

CLOTHING 3

Date of birth _____

A. Your jacket is beautiful.

B. I can make you one. Let me get your measurements.

اندازه گیری لباس پاس ص

My shoulders are _____.

My chest is _____.

My arm is _____.

My waist is _____.

My hips are _____.

CLOTHING 4

City _____

A. _____ is having a good sale on clothes this week.

B. What's on sale?

A. Sweaters and pajamas for kids.

B. I can't afford to buy anything this month. Maybe next month.

A. Let's go window shopping then.

CLOTHING 5

State _____

A. Can I help you?
B. No, thanks. I'm just looking.

A. Can I help you?
B. Yes, please. I'm looking for _____.

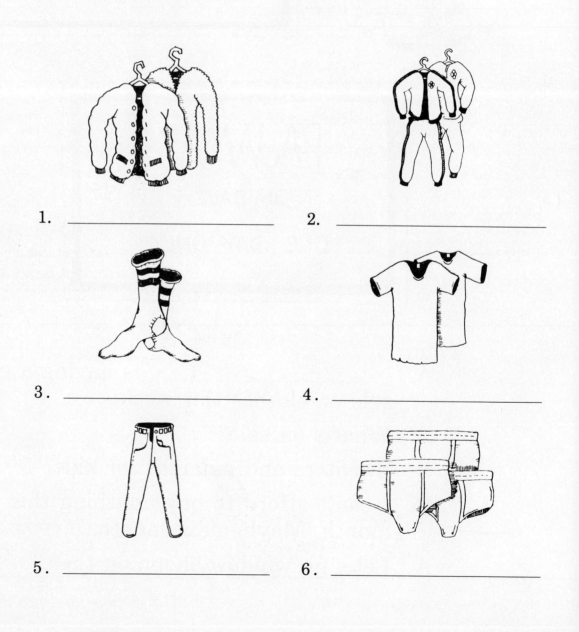

1. _____   2. _____

3. _____   4. _____

5. _____   6. _____

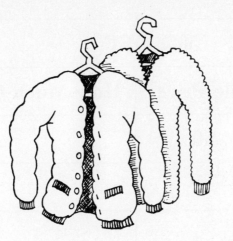

Sweaters $7.99 each,
reg. $9.99.
Many colors and styles.
Women's S-M-L.
Cotton-polyester knit.

1. What's on sale?
2. What colors can you buy?
3. What sizes can you buy?
4. What are they made of?
5. What's the regular price?
6. What's the sale price?
7. How much can you save?

50% off Men's and
Ladies' warm-ups.
Many styles and
colors. Polyester-
cotton. S-M-L-XL.
Regular $25.00–$30.00

1. What's the regular price?
2. What is the sale price?
3. How much can you save?

50% OFF		
Regular Price	**Sale Price**	**How Much Can You Save?**
$ 1.00	.50	.50
2.00		
3.00		
4.00		
5.00		
10.00		
15.00		
20.00		
25.00		
50.00		
100.00		

	Regular	Sale Price	Save!
	$16.00	$ 9.98	
	$12.00	$ 8.50	
	$ 9.00	$ 7.59	
	$15.99	$12.00	

1. What's the regular price of the _____ ?

2. What's the sale price of the _____ ?

3. How much can you save on the sweaters? _____

4. How much can you save on the jogging suits? _____

5. How much can you save on the sleepers? _____

6. How much can you save on the pants? _____

CLOTHING 6

Country _____

A. How do these pants look?
B. They look a little short.
A. You're right. I think I want a longer pair.
B. Here, try these on.

OPPOSITES

small _____

short _____

expensive _____

long _____

big _____

cheap _____

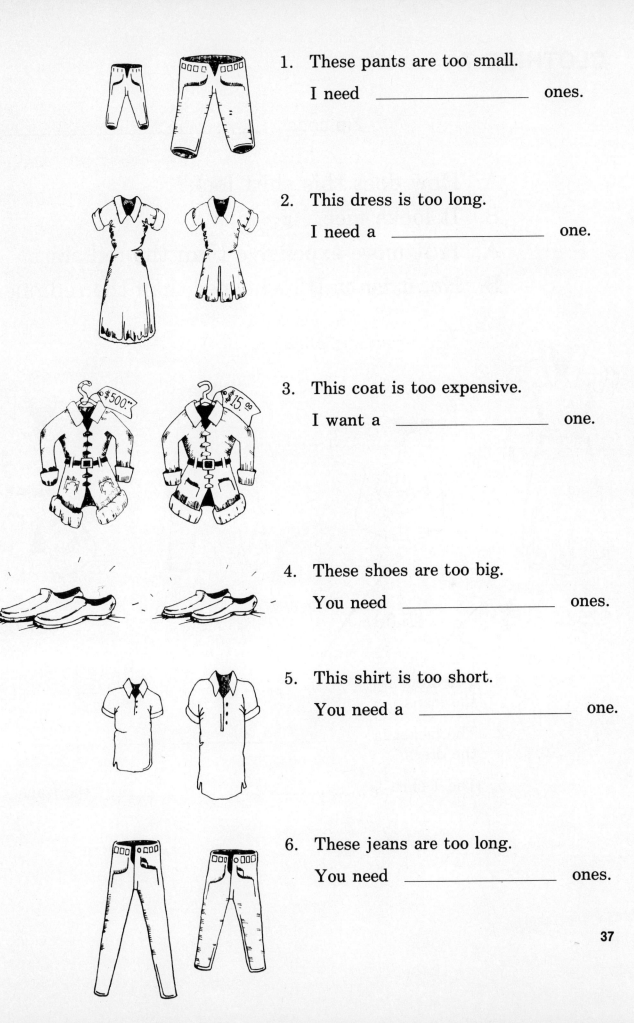

1. These pants are too small.

   I need _____ ones.

2. This dress is too long.

   I need a _____ one.

3. This coat is too expensive.

   I want a _____ one.

4. These shoes are too big.

   You need _____ ones.

5. This shirt is too short.

   You need a _____ one.

6. These jeans are too long.

   You need _____ ones.

CLOTHING 7

A. How does this shirt look?

B. It looks nice.

A. Is it more expensive than the red shirt?

B. No, it isn't. It's cheaper than the red one.

$25.00 $5.00 $17.50 $27.00

1. The dress is _____ _____ _____
   the jeans.

2. The jacket is _____ _____ _____
   the dress.

3. The T-shirt is _____ _____ the jeans.

**20% off
3 days only
entire stock**

**30% off
everything
this weekend**

**50%
clearance
sale**

Store A

Store B

Store C

1. Which store has the cheapest prices?
2. Which store has the best sale?
3. Which store has 1/2 off?
4. Which store has a three-day sale?
5. Which store has a sale on Saturday and Sunday?
6. Which store is the most expensive?

CLOTHING 8

In case of emergency call _____

name

A. Are you next?

B. Yes, I want this blanket.

A. Will this be all?

B. Yes.

A. It's $24 plus tax.

B. Oh. $24?

A. Yes.

B. I'm sorry. I thought it was $14.

A. Do you still want it?

B. No, thanks. That's too much.

A. No problem.

What does the price tag say?

1. _____ 2. _____ 3. _____

1.

2.

3.

4.

5.

6.

HAND WASH ONLY

buys
shrinks
take back

washes
takes back
read

washed	bought	shrank	took back
	take back	read	

Joni was happy to see the jeans. They were on the
clearance table. They were 50% off. She _____

them for her son. The jeans fit her son well. They were not too

big or too small. Then she _____ them. They

_____ a lot. They were too small. Joni

_____ the jeans _____ to the

store. The store manager didn't _____ them

_____ because Joni bought them on clearance

sale. Next time Joni will _____ the label.

1. Where did Joni see the jeans?
2. What happened to the jeans?
3. Who took the jeans back to the store?
4. Why didn't the store manager take them back?
5. What will Joni do next time she sees a clearance sale?

1. _____
2. _____
3. _____
4. _____

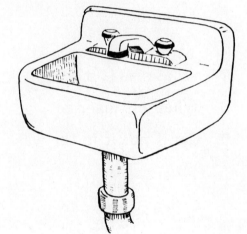

5. _____
6. _____
7. _____
8. _____

hand wash   preshrunk
machine wash   do not machine wash
cotton-polyester   wool
permanent press   silk

```
100% Wool
Product of USA
Hand wash only
M          10-12
```

1. What size is it? _____
2. What's it made of? _____
3. Can I put it in the washer? _____

```
Small
Machine Washable
Cotton-Polyester
Hong Kong
```

4. What size is it? _____
5. What's it made of? _____
6. Can I put it in the washer? _____

```
Ladies L
Hecho en Mexico
Do not machine wash
Silk
```

7. What size is it? _____
8. What's it made of? _____
9. Can I put it in the washer? _____

```
35% Cotton 65% Polyester
Machine Wash Warm
Made in Taiwan
Preshrunk
```

10. What size is it? _____
11. What's it made of? _____
12. Can I put it in the washer? _____

CLOTHING 9

In case of emergency call _____ .

number

A. Where are the sweatshirts?

B. Look upstairs in the sportswear department.

A. Is the shoe department upstairs too?

B. No, it isn't. It's downstairs.

A. Thanks.

Match

baby clothes	sportswear dept.
shoes	baby dept.
sweatshirts	shoe dept.
towels	jewelry dept.
watches	housewares dept.
tables	furniture dept.

_ FLOOR

_ FLOOR

_ FLOOR

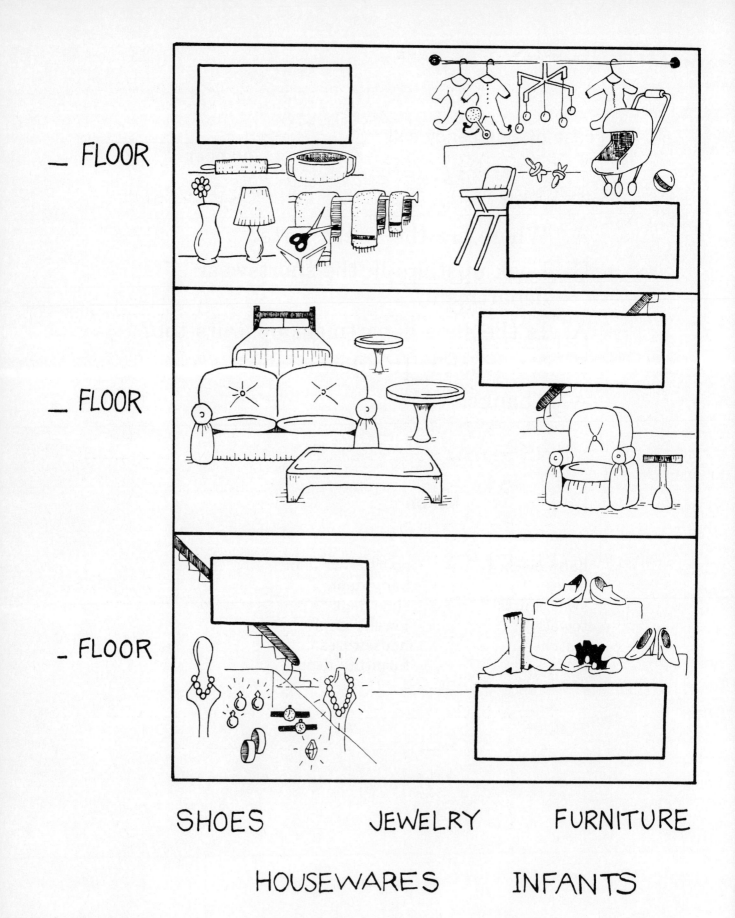

SHOES   JEWELRY   FURNITURE

HOUSEWARES   INFANTS

46

1. Where are the boots?

   They're in the _____ department on the

   _____ floor.

2. Where are the watches?

   They're in the _____ department on the

   _____ floor.

3. Where are the shoes?

   They're in the _____

   _____ on the _____

   _____ .

4. Where are the chairs?

   They're in the _____

   _____ on the _____

   _____ .

5. Where are the towels?

   They're in the _____ _____

   on the _____ _____ .

6. Where are the baby sleepers?

   They're in the _____ _____

   on the _____ _____ .

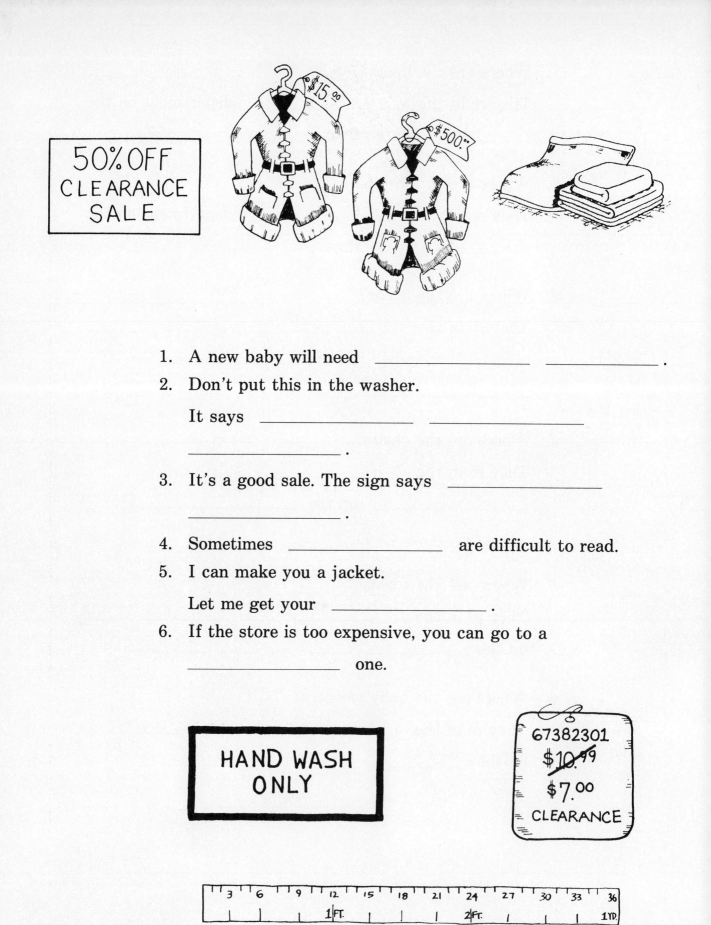

1. A new baby will need _____ _____ .

2. Don't put this in the washer.

   It says _____ _____

   _____ .

3. It's a good sale. The sign says _____

   _____ .

4. Sometimes _____ are difficult to read.

5. I can make you a jacket.

   Let me get your _____ .

6. If the store is too expensive, you can go to a

   _____ one.

3

FOOD

First name _____

A. What's on sale this week?
B. Look at the ad.

PRICES EFFECTIVE WEDNESDAY JULY 23 THRU THURSDAY JULY 29
J.G. GROCERY
WE ACCEPT U.S.D.A. FOOD STAMPS

A. Do you see fish and diet soda?
B. Yes, they're on special.
The fish is _____ a pound.
The diet soda is _____ a six-pack.

The sign says:

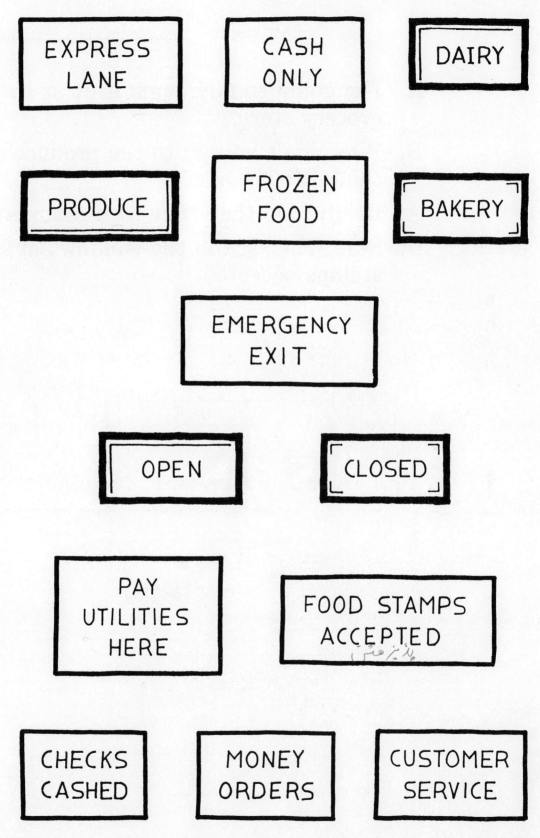

EXPRESS LANE

CASH ONLY

DAIRY

PRODUCE

FROZEN FOOD

BAKERY

EMERGENCY EXIT

OPEN

CLOSED

PAY UTILITIES HERE

FOOD STAMPS ACCEPTED

CHECKS CASHED

MONEY ORDERS

CUSTOMER SERVICE

FOOD 2

Last name _____

A. I'm going to buy some fruit at the grocery store.

B. Why don't you go to the produce store? I think it's cheaper.

A. Really? Do they take food stamps?

B. Sure. The sign in the window says food stamps accepted.

1. cheap _____

2. big _____

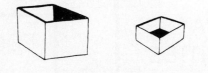

3. small _____

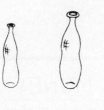

4. large _____

Joe is going to the produce store. He's going to buy some bananas and apples. He thinks the produce store is cheaper than the grocery store. He thinks the fruits and vegetables are fresher, too.

1. Is Joe going to the produce store?

   _____

2. Does he think the produce store is cheaper than the grocery store?

   _____

3. Does he think the produce store has fresher fruits and vegetables too?

   _____

4. Do you go to a produce store?

   _____

5. Do you think the produce store has fresher fruits and vegetables?

   _____

6. Do you think the produce store is cheaper than the grocery store?

   _____

FOOD 3

I'm from _____ .

A. This line is the shortest. Let's get in it.
B. We can't. The sign says ten items or less.
A. You're right. We have too many things.

More or Less

1. $10.00 is _____ than $9.00.

2. $1.00 is _____ than $.50.

3. $9.98 is _____ than $9.89.

4. $36.00 is _____ than $37.00.

5. $50.38 is _____ than $53.08.

6. $29.00 is _____ than $28.99.

7. $99.00 is _____ than $100.00.

8. $47.33 is _____ than $46.00.

9. $100.00 is _____ than $50.00.

10. $500.00 is _____ than $5.00.

11. $91.00 is _____ than $19.00.

12. $65.00 is _____ than $6.50.

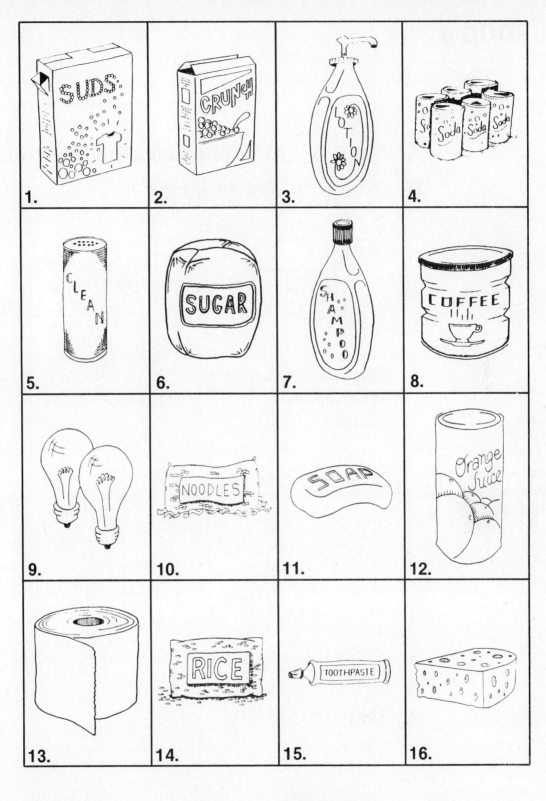

detergent   cereal   hand lotion   soda
cleanser   sugar   shampoo   coffee
light bulbs   noodles   soap   orange juice
toilet paper   rice   toothpaste   cheese

FOOD 4

Address _____

A. This bread is cheaper than that one.
B. But this loaf is larger.

1. Which one is cheaper?

_____

2. Which one is fresher?

_____

56

FOOD 5

A. Excuse me. Where's the shampoo?

B. It's on aisle 12 near the hand lotion.

A. I looked on aisle 12, but I didn't see it.

B. It's on the top shelf near the end.

A. Thanks. I'll look again.

FOOD 6

A. Is this diet soda on sale?

B. No, it's not.

A. Where can I find the soda that's on sale?

B. It's over there. It's next to the caffeine-free soda.

A. Thanks.

Match

caffeine free   no salt
low sodium   no sugar
sugar free   no caffeine
diet
decaffeinated
low calorie

Age _____

A. Where's the detergent that's on special?

B. On aisle 2.

A. Are the rebate forms there too?

B. No, they're not. The rebate forms are at the customer service desk.

A. Thanks.

J G
GROCERY

DETERGENT...4.50

ORANGES....1.00

PAPER........59

COOKIES.....1.29

TOTAL   7.38

CASH.......10.00

CHANGE....2.62

THANK YOU

$ 2.00 REBATE

SEND IN THIS FORM WITH
THE RECEIPT AND THE
UPC SYMBOL FROM KLEEN.

NAME:_____
ADDRESS:_____
_____

4567|

456790

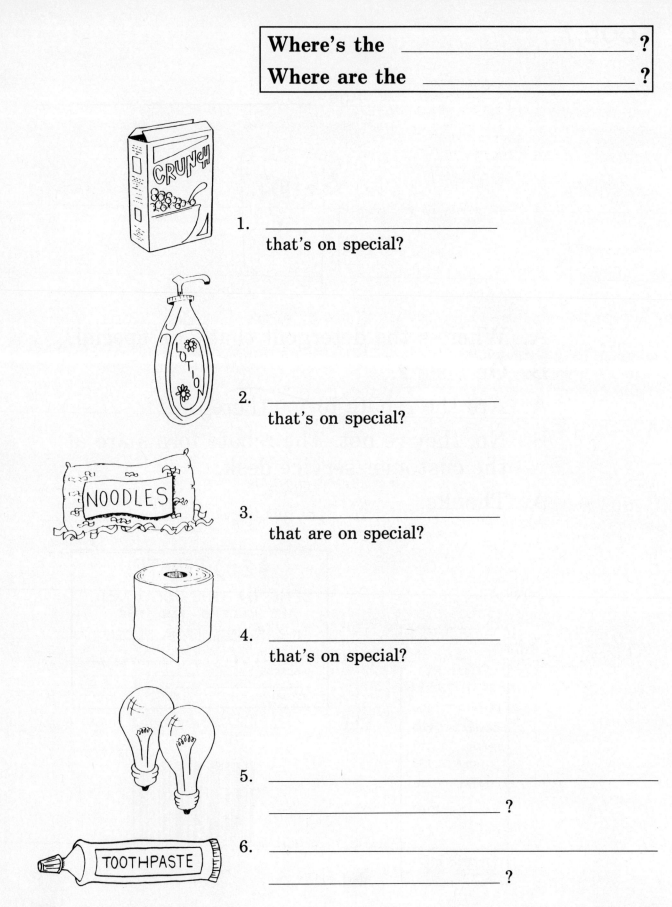

| Where's the | _____ | ? |
| Where are the | _____ | ? |

1. _____

   that's on special?

2. _____

   that's on special?

3. _____

   that are on special?

4. _____

   that's on special?

5. _____

   _____ ?

6. _____

   _____ ?

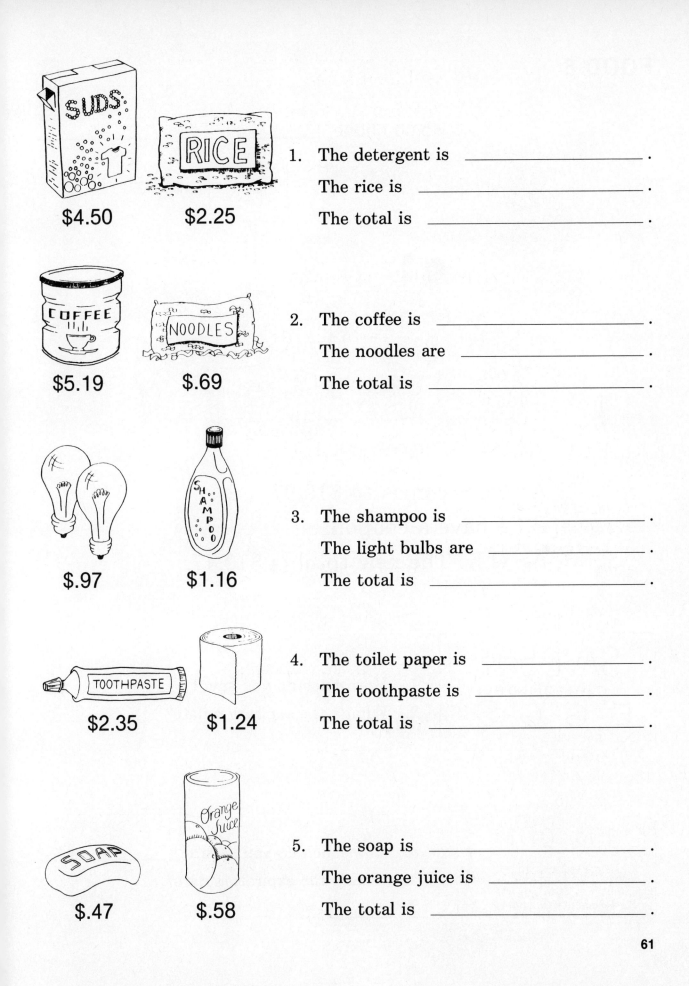

$4.50 $2.25

1. The detergent is _____.

   The rice is _____.

   The total is _____.

$5.19 $.69

2. The coffee is _____.

   The noodles are _____.

   The total is _____.

$.97 $1.16

3. The shampoo is _____.

   The light bulbs are _____.

   The total is _____.

$2.35 $1.24

4. The toilet paper is _____.

   The toothpaste is _____.

   The total is _____.

$.47 $.58

5. The soap is _____.

   The orange juice is _____.

   The total is _____.

FOOD 8

A. That comes to $10.97.

B. I have a coupon.

A. O.K. The new total is $10.47.

1. How much do you save? _____
2. What's the expiration date?

   _____

3. How much do you save? _____
4. What's the expiration date?

   _____

62

FOOD 9

A. Excuse me. I think there's a mistake here.

B. What's the problem?

A. Does this say $4.19 for bananas?

B. Oh, no. You bought a little more than four pounds. The bananas were $1.05.

A. Thanks for your time.

B. If you have more questions, please ask.

HAPPY MARKET

4.19 lb bananas	@	4/100	1.05
2 lb apples	@	3/100	.67
3.50 lb oranges	@	2/100	1.75
		Total	3.47

Have a Nice Day

```
              HAPPY SUPERMARKET
                8527 MAIN ST.
                4-8   9:12 A.M.


4.19 lb          @   4/100
bananas                                1.05
meat                                   2.31
meat                                   2.64
orange juice                            .69

                     Total            6.69
                     Eligible         6.69
                     Cash due          .00
                     Stamp TND.      10.00

                .31 change
                3.00 food stamp change


           You Get a Good Deal
```

1. What's the total? _____

2. What's the total eligible for food

   stamps? _____

3. How much change in cash is there? _____

4. How much change in food stamps? _____

FOOD 10

Date _____

A. Let's dye some eggs.

B. What do we need?

A. We need

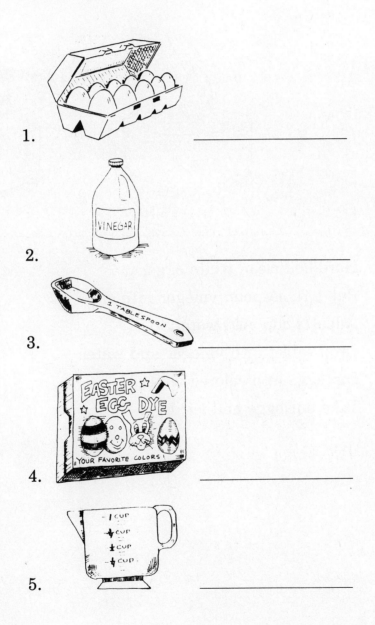

1. _____

2. _____

3. _____

4. _____

5. _____

Making Easter Eggs

 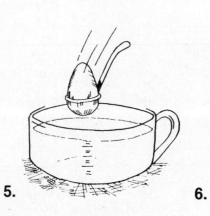 

1. Hard-boil clean white eggs.
2. Put 1 tablespoon vinegar into cup.
3. Add 1/2 cup cold water.
4. Drop tablet into vinegar and water.
5. Dip eggs into colored water.
6. Take out eggs and let dry.

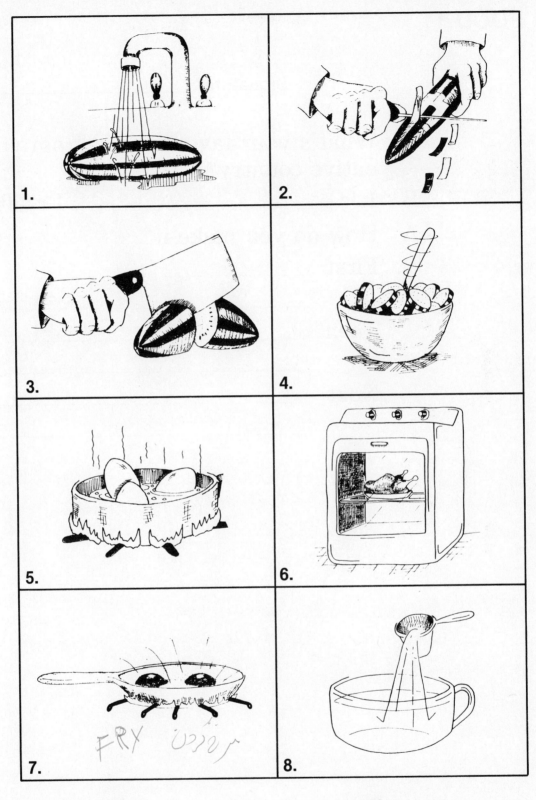

1.
2.
3.
4.
5.
6.
7. FRY بسرخ کردن
8.

wash
chop or cut
boil
fry سرخ کردن

peel
stir or mix
bake
pour or add

FOOD 11

Signature _____

A. What's your favorite food from your native country?

B. It's _____ . I really like it.

A. How do you make it?

B. First _____

_____ .

Then _____

_____ .

Next _____

_____ .

FOOD 12

Favorite food _____

A. I bought this milk yesterday, but it's sour.

B. What's the date on the carton?

A. It's January 17.

B. I think you should return it. Today is only the fourteenth.

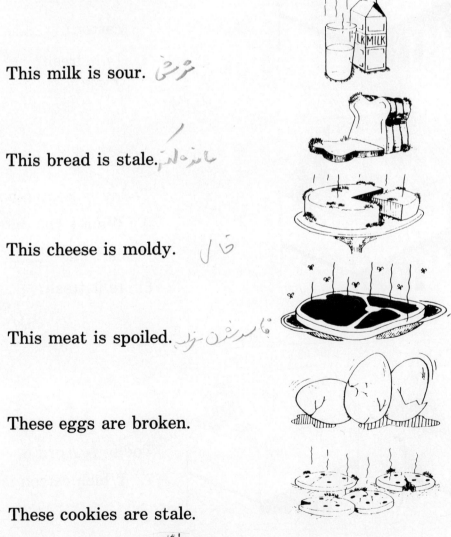

This milk is sour. مرشى

This bread is stale. خبز بايت

This cheese is moldy. قالب

This meat is spoiled. لحم فاسد

These eggs are broken.

These cookies are stale.

كى

Today is March 10.

1. What's the date on the carton? _____

2. Is it fresh? _____

Today is November 22.

3. What's the date on the carton? _____

4. Is it fresh? _____

Today is September 3.

5. What's the date on the carton? _____

6. Is it fresh? _____

Today is April 6.

7. Which carton is fresher?

_____

NO
CAFFEINE

J G
GROCERY

DETERGENT...4.50
ORANGES....1.00
PAPER.......59
COOKIES.....1.29
TOTAL   7.38
CASH......10.00
CHANGE....2.62

THANK YOU

SAVE 50¢
CARTON OF
E G G S
EXPIRES MAY 12

1. If you buy _____ _____ ,
   return it.

2. _____ is my favorite food from my native
   country.

3. Always remember to check your _____ .

4. If you can't have caffeine, look for the sign

   _____ _____ .

5. You can save a little money if you remember to use a

   _____ .

6. Let's read the _____ to see what's on sale.

38¢   51¢ $2.29 $1.59
              LB.

PRICES EFFECTIVE WEDNESDAY
JULY 23 THRU THURSDAY JULY 29

J.G. GROCERY

WE ACCEPT U.S.D.A. FOOD STAMPS

71

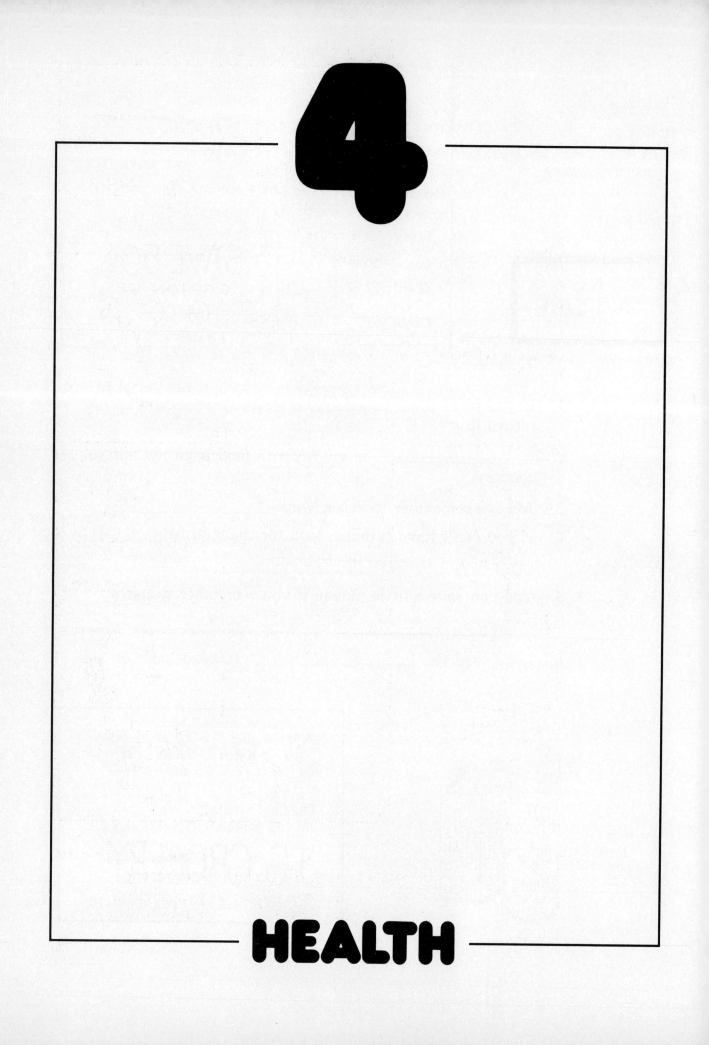

4

HEALTH

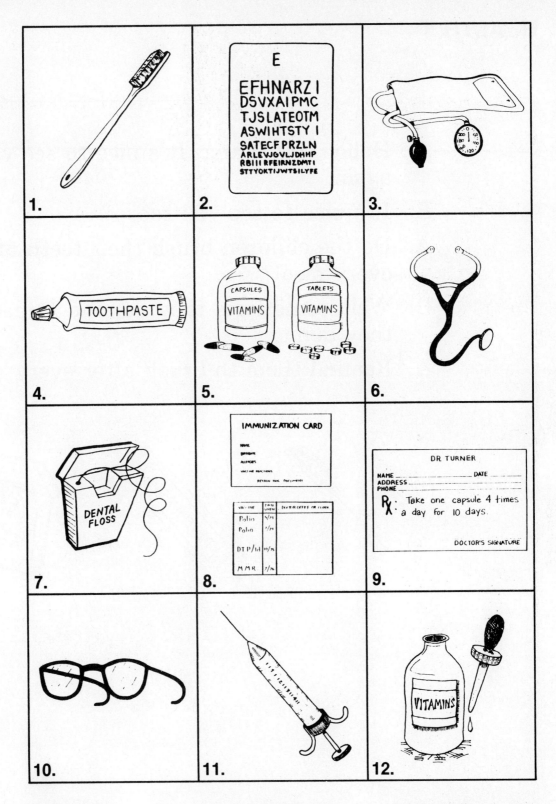

1.

2. E
EFHNARZI
DSVXAIPMC
TJSLATEOTM
ASWIHTSTYI
SATECFPRZLN
ARLEWGVLJDHHP
RBIIIRFEIRNZDMTI
STTYOKTIJWTSILYFE

3.

4. TOOTHPASTE

5. CAPSULES VITAMINS / TABLETS VITAMINS

6.

7. DENTAL FLOSS

8. IMMUNIZATION CARD
NAME
BIRTHDATE
ALLERGIES
VACCINE REACTIONS
RETAIN THIS DOCUMENT

VACCINE	DATE GIVEN	DOCTOR OFFICE OR CLINIC
Polio	5/74	
Polio	7/74	
DTP/Td	10/75	
MMR	7/76	

9. DR TURNER
NAME _____ DATE _____
ADDRESS _____
PHONE _____
℞ Take one capsule 4 times a day for 10 days.
DOCTOR'S SIGNATURE

10.

11.

12. VITAMINS

toothbrush   eye chart   blood pressure cuff
toothpaste   vitamins, capsules, tablets   stethoscope
dental floss   immunization record   prescription
glasses   shot needle   vitamin drops

Name _____

A. Hello, Mrs. Vang. It's nice to see you again.

B. It's nice to see you too.

A. Do the children brush their teeth after every meal?

B. Well, sometimes they do, and sometimes they don't.

A. Remind them to brush after every meal.

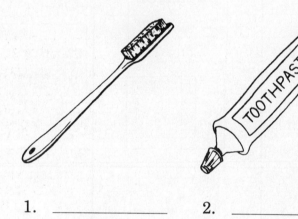 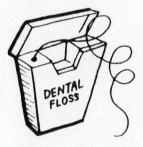

1. _____   2. _____   3. _____

Zip code _____

A. Why are you squinting?

B. I can't see very well. Everything looks blurry.

A. Maybe you need glasses.

B. Where can I get them?

A. Make an appointment with an eye doctor.

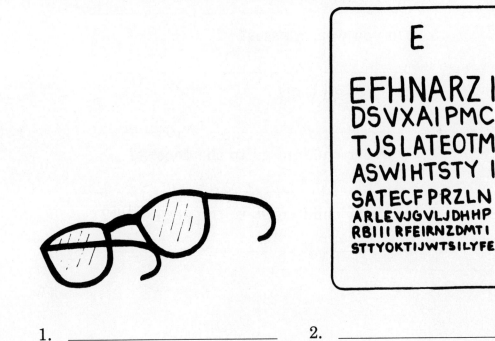

1. _____   2. _____

Yes,	I we they	do.

No,	I we they	don't.

1. Do you go to the dentist?

   —————— , —————— —————— .

2. Do you have cavities?

   —————— , —————— —————— .

3. Do you like to go to the dentist?

   —————— , —————— —————— .

4. Do you go to the eye doctor?

   —————— , —————— —————— .

5. Do you wear glasses?

   —————— , —————— —————— .

6. Do you see well?

   —————— , —————— —————— .

7. Do your children go to the dentist?

   —————— , —————— —————— .

8. Do your children go to the eye doctor?

   —————— , —————— —————— .

HEALTH 3

A. Your son should take vitamins.

B. Vitamins? Will they make him fat?

A. No, they won't. They're important for his health.

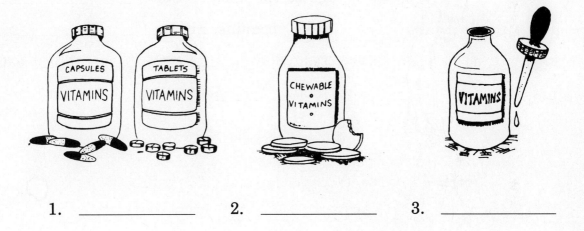

1. _____   2. _____   3. _____

He is tired. He _____

rest. He _____

not smoke. He

_____ eat good food.

She is pregnant. She _____

go to the doctor. She _____

take vitamins. She _____

rest. She _____ eat good

food.

1. Should she take vitamins?

   _____ , _____ _____ .

2. Should he stop smoking?

   _____ , _____ _____ .

3. Should she rest?

   _____ , _____ _____ .

4. Should she eat good food?

   _____ , _____ _____ .

| should |
| shouldn't |

1. I have a fever.

   You _____ go to school.

   You _____ put on a sweater.

   You _____ drink orange juice.

2. I have a cold.

   You _____ wear a sweater.

   You _____ rest.

   You _____ kiss a baby.

3. I feel dizzy.

   You _____ rest.

   You _____ drive.

   You _____ tell your doctor.

HEALTH 4

Telephone _____

A. Hello. This is

Miss	
Mrs.	_____ .
Mr.	
Ms.	

I need to make an appointment.

B. That's fine. What for?

A. My | son
daughter | needs a physical.

B. Can you come Tuesday the twenty-first at 3:00?

A. Tuesday the twenty-first at 3:00?
Yes, I can.

MAY

SUN	MON	TUE	WED	THU	FRI	SAT
			1	2	3	4
5	6	7	8	9	10	11
12	13	14	15	16	17	18
19	20	21	22	23	24	25
26	27	28	29	30	31	

a physical
an examination
a checkup

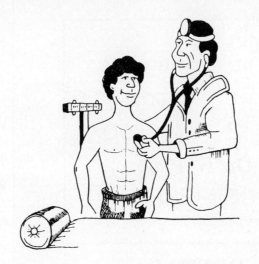

---

an injection
a shot

---

a vaccination
an immunization

---

a vaccination record
an immunization record

IMMUNIZATION CARD	VACCINE	DATE GIVEN	DOCTOR OFFICE OR CLINIC
NAME:	Polio	5/74	
BIRTHDATE:	Polio	7/74	
ALLERGIES:			
VACCINE REACTIONS:	DTP/Td	10/75	
RETAIN THIS DOCUMENT	MMR	7/76	

---

1. A physical is the same as a _____ .

2. An immunization is the same as a _____ .

3. An immunization record is the same as a _____

   _____ .

4. A checkup is the same as an _____ .

5. A shot is the same as an _____ .

6. A vaccination record is the same as an _____

   _____ .

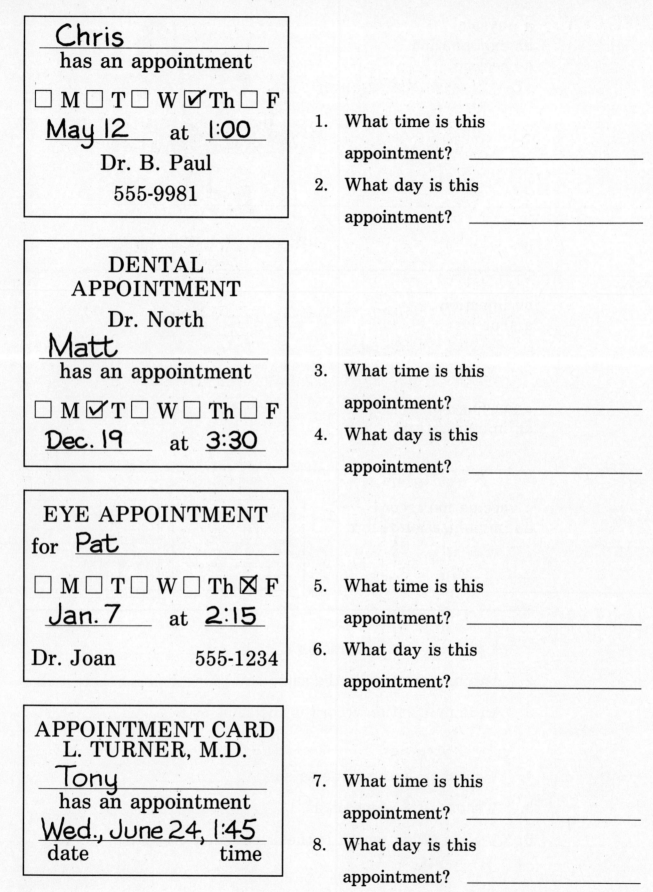

Chris

has an appointment

☐ M ☐ T ☐ W ☑ Th ☐ F

May 12   at 1:00

Dr. B. Paul

555-9981

1. What time is this
   appointment? _____
2. What day is this
   appointment? _____

DENTAL
APPOINTMENT

Dr. North

Matt

has an appointment

☐ M ☑ T ☐ W ☐ Th ☐ F

Dec. 19   at 3:30

3. What time is this
   appointment? _____
4. What day is this
   appointment? _____

EYE APPOINTMENT

for Pat

☐ M ☐ T ☐ W ☐ Th ☒ F

Jan. 7   at 2:15

Dr. Joan   555-1234

5. What time is this
   appointment? _____
6. What day is this
   appointment? _____

APPOINTMENT CARD
L. TURNER, M.D.

Tony

has an appointment

Wed., June 24, 1:45

date   time

7. What time is this
   appointment? _____
8. What day is this
   appointment? _____

HEALTH 5

A. Good morning. We need to complete this form.

B. O.K.

A. Have you ever had the chicken pox?

B. Yes, I have.

A. Have you ever had the measles?

B. No, I haven't.

A. Have you ever had heart problems?

B. I'm not sure.

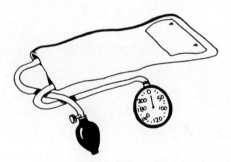

1. _____

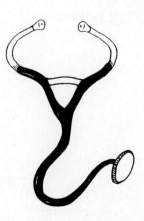

2. _____

NEW PATIENT FORM

Patient's name: _____

                                        Last   First

Age _____ Birthdate _____ Sex _____

Patient's address: _____

                      Number   Street   City   State   Zip code

---

Please [✔] if you have ever had:

☐	chicken pox کلرامان	☐	allergies
☐	measles سرخچه	☐	polio
☐	mumps اوریون	☐	TB
☐	rubella	☐	diabetes
☐	high blood pressure		

Please [✔] if you have ever been treated for:

☐	heart problems	☐	liver problems
☐	lung problems	☐	bladder problems
☐	kidney problems	☐	stomach problems
	☐	other _____	

Have you ever had an operation? ☐ yes   When? _____
                                          ☐ no

Are you taking medicine now? ☐ yes
                                       ☐ no

Name of medicine _____

Do you have insurance? ☐ yes
                           ☐ no

Name of insurance _____

_____   _____
        Signature   Date

Have you ever had	chicken pox?	measles?	mumps?	polio?	TB? (Tuberculosis)	allergies?
	yes no	yes no	yes no	yes no	yes no	yes no
	yes no	yes no	yes no	yes no	yes no	yes no
	yes no	yes no	yes no	yes no	yes no	yes no
	yes no	yes no	yes no	yes no	yes no	yes no

*See Teacher's Guide

1. How many people had chicken pox?
2. How many people had measles?
3. How many people had mumps?
4. How many people had polio?
5. How many people had TB?
6. How many people had allergies?

HEALTH 6

A. What's wrong? You look sick.

B. Oh, I have a headache.

A. Would you like an aspirin?

B. No thanks. I think I'm allergic to aspirin.

A. You should tell your doctor.

I You We They	think

He She	thinks

1. _____ _____ I'm allergic.

2. _____ _____ she's pregnant.

3. _____ _____ he has an ulcer.

HEALTH 7

Native country _____

A. Do you have any allergies?

B. Yes, I do. I'm allergic to dust.
   I get really sick.

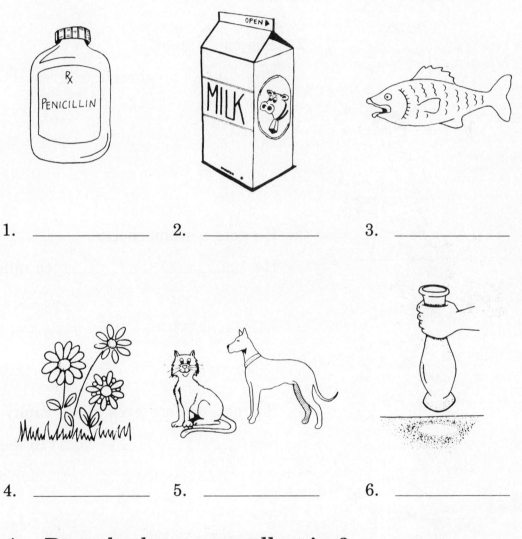

1. _____   2. _____   3. _____

4. _____   5. _____   6. _____

A. Does he have any allergies?

B. Yes, he does. He's allergic to milk. He
   gets a stomachache.

1. He gets a rash.

   He _____ allergic to penicillin.

2. She can't breathe.

   She _____ allergic to grass.

3. He gets a stomachache.

   He _____ _____ to milk.

4. She gets watery eyes and a runny nose.

   She _____ _____ to animals.

5. She sneezes.

   _____ _____ _____ to dust.

1. He's allergic to penicillin.

   He _____ .

2. She's allergic to grass and flowers.

   She _____ .

3. He's allergic to milk.

   He _____ .

4. She's allergic to animals.

   She _____ .

5. She's allergic to dust.

   She _____ .

Age _____

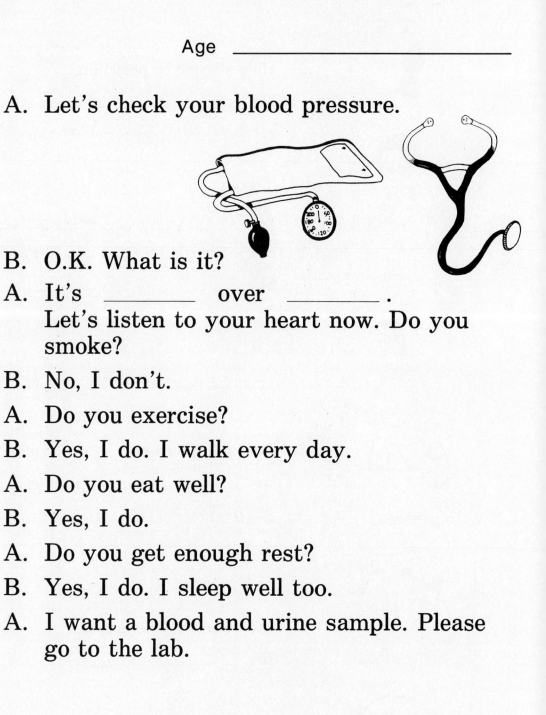

A. Let's check your blood pressure.

B. O.K. What is it?

A. It's _____ over _____ .
Let's listen to your heart now. Do you smoke?

B. No, I don't.

A. Do you exercise?

B. Yes, I do. I walk every day.

A. Do you eat well?

B. Yes, I do.

A. Do you get enough rest?

B. Yes, I do. I sleep well too.

A. I want a blood and urine sample. Please go to the lab.

HEALTH 9

A. You have an infection. Have you ever had penicillin?

B. I'm not sure.

A. I'm giving you a prescription for penicillin. Take it four times a day for ten days.

B. How much?

A. One capsule.

B. O.K. One capsule four times a day for ten days.

1. Take it:
   1. in the morning
   2. at noon
   3. in the afternoon
   4. at night

2. Take it:
Monday	Saturday
Tuesday	Sunday
Wednesday	Monday
Thursday	Tuesday
Friday	Wednesday

teaspoon—tsp. or t.	hours—hrs.
tablespoon—Tbl. or T.	week—wk.
one time—once	two times—twice

1. t<u>eas</u>poon _____

2. T<u>a</u>blespoon _____

3. t<u>ea</u>spoon _____

4. T<u>a</u>blespoon _____

5. h<u>ou</u>rs _____

6. w<u>ee</u>k _____

7. one time _____

8. two times _____

| 1 T.
once a day | How much? _____
When? _____ |

| 2 tsp.
every 4 hrs. | How much? _____
When? _____ |

```
┌─────────────────┐
│ 2 tsp.          │     1.   How much?  _____
│ every 4 hrs.    │     2.   When?      _____
│ for 3 days      │     3.   How long?  _____
└─────────────────┘
```

```
┌─────────────────┐
│ 1 capsule       │     4.   How much?  _____
│ every morning   │     5.   When?      _____
│ for 10 days     │     6.   How long?  _____
└─────────────────┘
```

```
┌─────────────────┐
│ 1 T. every      │     7.   How much?  _____
│ 6 hrs. for      │     8.   When?      _____
│ 1 wk.           │     9.   How long?  _____
└─────────────────┘
```

```
┌─────────────────┐
│ 1 tablet        │    10.   How much?  _____
│ twice a day     │    11.   When?      _____
│ for 14 days     │    12.   How long?  _____
└─────────────────┘
```

```
┌─────────────────┐
│ 1/2 tsp. in     │    13.   How much?  _____
│ the morning     │    14.   When?      _____
│ for 10 days     │    15.   How long?  _____
└─────────────────┘
```

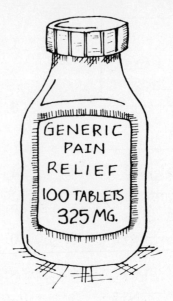

Medicine Directions: Acetaminophen *Dosage*: Adults 1 or 2 tablets every 4–6 hours. Children 6–12 1 tablet. Children under 6 call a doctor. *Warning*: Do not exceed 12 tablets a day. Do not drive if drowsy. Consult your doctor if pregnant.

1. My father has a headache. How many tablets should he take? _____

2. My two-year-old daughter has a fever. How many should she take? _____

3. His wife has a backache. How many should she take?

   _____

4. My friend has a headache, but she's pregnant. How many should she take? _____

HEALTH 10

City _____

A. My ear hurts.

B. How long has it hurt?

A. About one week.

B. You have an ear infection. Are you allergic to any medicine?

A. No, I'm not.

B. Do you take any other medicine?

A. I take vitamins.

Do you take medicine?	What medicine do you take?	Why do you take it?

HEALTH 11

Have you ever had chicken pox? yes ☐

no ☐

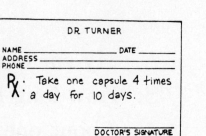

A. Did you go to the doctor?

B. Yes, I did.

A. What's the matter?

B. I have an ear infection.

A. Did you get a prescription?

B. Yes. I have to go to the pharmacy now.

A. How long do you have to take the medicine?

B. I have to take it for ten days. Then I have to see the doctor again.

1. I have an ear infection.

2. I _____ _____ _____ to the pharmacy.

3. I _____ _____ _____ some medicine.

4. I _____ _____ _____ it for ten days.

5. Then I _____ _____ _____ the doctor again.

```
┌─────────────────────────────────────────────────┐
│                 DR. TURNER                      │
│                                                 │
│  NAME _____ DATE _____  │
│  ADDRESS _____  │
│  PHONE _____  │
│                                                 │
│  R : Take one capsule 4 times                   │
│   X   a day for 10 days.                        │
│                                                 │
│                                                 │
│                                                 │
│                         _____     │
│                          DOCTOR'S SIGNATURE     │
└─────────────────────────────────────────────────┘
```

1. How much do you take?

   _____

2. When do you take it?

   _____

3. How many days do you take it?

   _____

go   see

take   stay

drink

1. I have an ear infection.

   _____ _____ _____ _____ to the doctor.

   _____ _____ _____ _____ medicine.

2. He has a bladder infection.

   _____ _____ _____ _____ to the doctor.

   _____ _____ _____ _____ medicine.

3. My children have the chicken pox.

   _____ _____ _____ _____ inside.

   _____ _____ _____ rest.

4. La is pregnant.

   _____ _____ _____ _____ the doctor.

   _____ _____ _____ rest.

5. Sam has a fever.

   _____ _____ _____ _____ water.

   _____ _____ _____ rest.

Date of birth _____

A. I need to see the doctor again.

B. When?

A. In ten days.

B. O.K. How is Monday at 9:30?

A. Oh, that's not convenient.

B. O.K. How about Monday at 11:00?

A. That's not convenient either. Can I come in the afternoon?

B. Let's see. How about Monday at 2:15?

A. O.K. Monday at 2:15 is fine.

1. It's on _____ at _____ .

2. It's on _____ at _____ .

3. It's on _____ at _____ .

4. It's on _____ at _____ .

State _____

Emergency Room

A. My son stepped on a nail.

B. Has he ever had a tetanus shot?

A. I don't know.

B. It's important. Do you have his immunization record?

A. Yes, I do. Here it is.

B. His tetanus shot was over ten years ago. He needs another one.

IMMUNIZATION CARD

NAME: _____

BIRTHDATE: _____

ALLERGIES: _____

VACCINE REACTIONS: _____

RETAIN THIS DOCUMENT

VACCINE	DATE GIVEN	DOCTOR OFFICE OR CLINIC
Polio	5/74	
Polio	7/74	
DTP/Td	10/75	
MMR	7/76	

Country _____

A. I can't come to school for a few weeks.

B. Oh, why not?

A. I'm going to have an operation.

B. What kind?

A. I'm going to have an eye operation.

B. I hope it's nothing serious.

A. My doctor says it's routine.

B. I'm glad to hear that.

routine	serious

1. A checkup is _____ .

2. Heart surgery is _____ .

3. A cut finger is _____ .

4. A blood sample is _____ .

5. Cancer surgery is _____ .

6. A high fever is _____ .

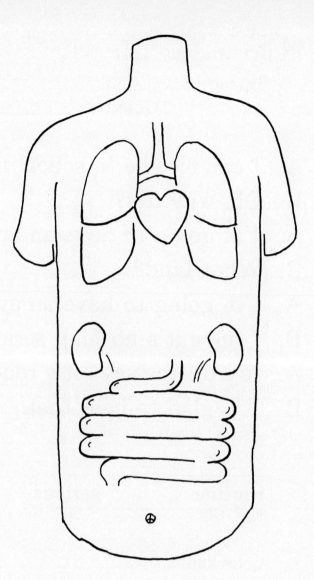

1. He's _____ __ __ _____ __ _____

    __ _____ kidneys.

2. She's _____ __ _____ __ __ _____

    __ _____ lungs.

3. He's _____ __ _____ __ _____

    __ _____ heart.

4. She's _____ __ _____ __ __ _____

    __ _____ intestines.

5. I had an operation on my _____ .

I'm glad to hear that.
I'm sorry to hear that.

1. My doctor says it's serious.

   _____ _____ _____ _____ _____ .

2. My doctor says it's routine.

   _____ _____ _____ _____ _____ .

3. My friend has a new baby.

   _____ _____ _____ _____ _____ .

4. My friend is in the hospital.

   _____ _____ _____ _____ _____ .

5. Her daughter has some cavities.

   _____ _____ _____ _____ _____ .

6. His daughter has allergies.

   _____ _____ _____ _____ _____ .

7. Her husband needs an operation.

   _____ _____ _____ _____ _____ .

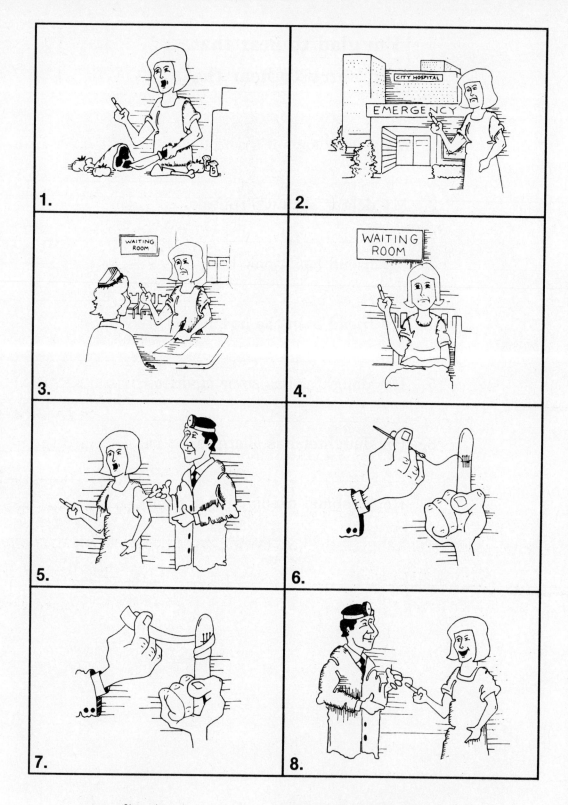

cuts finger
fills out form
gets a tetanus shot
bandages stitches

goes to emergency room
waits
gets stitches
comes back to get the stitches out

| went | bandaged | got | cut |
| waited | come back | filled | |

Ka _____ her finger last week. It was bleeding a lot. She _____ to the emergency room. When she was in the emergency room, she _____ out a form. The emergency room was very busy and Ka _____ a long time. The doctor looked at her finger. It was a bad cut. Ka _____ a tetanus shot. She _____ about ten stitches too. The doctor _____ her stitches to keep them clean. Ka will _____ _____ in a week to get the stitches out.

1. Who cut her finger?
2. Where did she go?
3. What did she fill out in the emergency room?
4. When does she have to go back to have the stitches taken out?
5. Why did Ka have a tetanus shot?

IMMUNIZATION CARD

NAME: _____

BIRTHDATE: _____

ALLERGIES: _____

VACCINE REACTIONS: _____

RETAIN THIS DOCUMENT

VACCINE	DATE GIVEN	DOCTOR OFFICE OR CLINIC
Polio	5/74	
Polio	7/74	
DTP/Td	10/75	
MMR	7/76	

1. Sometimes _____ can help you see better.

2. Keep your children's _____ _____ in a safe place.

3. What is your _____ _____ ?

   It's _____ over _____ .

4. _____ are important for good health.

5. You have to go to the pharmacy to buy a _____ .

6. If you think you are _____ , see a doctor.

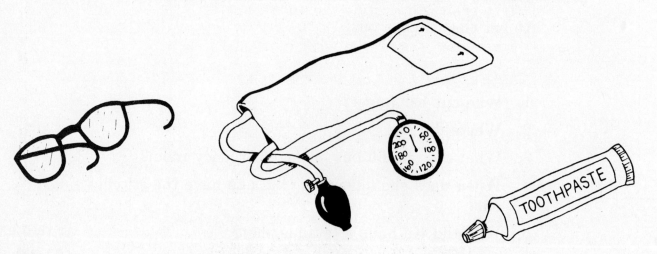

5

HOUSING

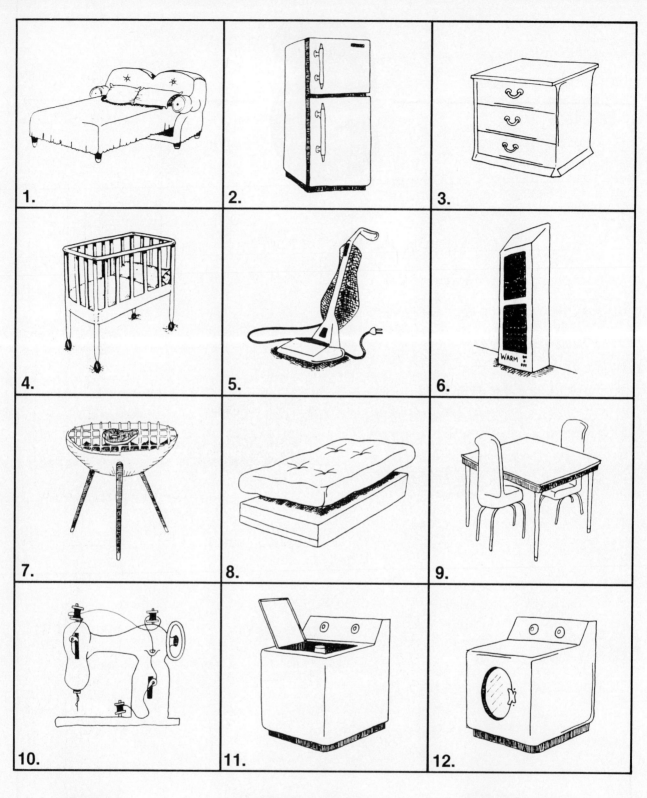

sofa bed	refrigerator	dresser
crib	vacuum	heater
barbecue	mattress/box spring	table and chairs
sewing machine	washer	dryer

HOUSING 1

A. I need a new stove.

B. Why?

A. My old one is broken.

B. Why don't you buy a used one?

1. _____

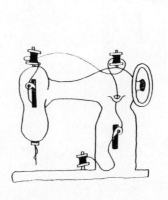

2. _____

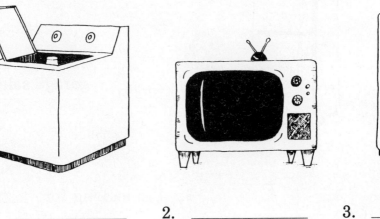

3. _____

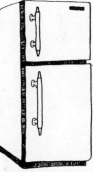

4. _____

5. _____

6. _____

HOUSING 2

Age _____

A. I'm looking for a used TV.
B. I saw one at the thrift store.
A. How much was it?
B. I think it was $75.

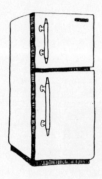

1. I'm looking for a used

_____ .

2. _____ _____ _____ _____

_____ garage sale.

3. I'm looking for _____ _____

_____ _____ .

4. _____ _____ _____ _____

_____ used furniture store.

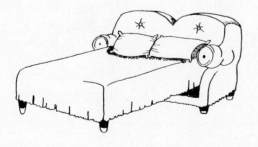

5. I'm looking for _____ _____

_____ .

6. _____ _____ _____ _____

_____ discount store.

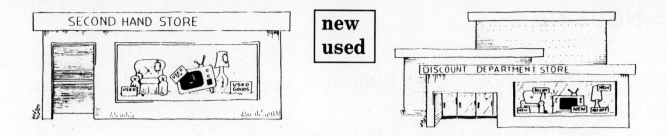

SECOND HAND STORE

new
used

DISCOUNT DEPARTMENT STORE

1. You can buy a _____ sofa bed at a thrift store.

2. You can buy a _____ vacuum at a garage sale.

3. You can buy a _____ mattress at a department store.

4. You can buy a _____ sewing machine at a rummage sale.

5. You can buy a _____ refrigerator at a discount store.

6. You can buy a _____ dresser at a flea market.

7. You can buy a _____ crib at a second-hand store.

8. You can buy a _____ washing machine at a garage sale.

Birthday _____

A. How much do you want for the sofa bed?

B. $50.

A. Will you take $40?

B. How about $45?

A. O.K.

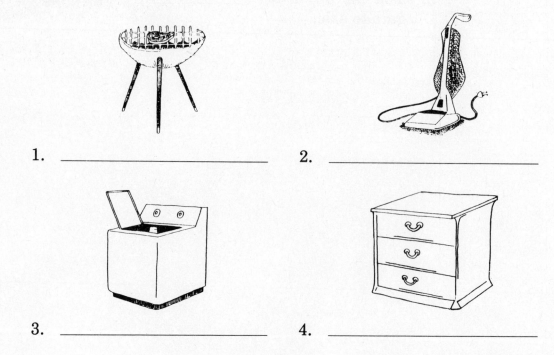

1. _____ 2. _____

3. _____ 4. _____

came
had

was
wanted

wanted   had

came   was

Xay _____ home from work at 10:00 last night. A stranger _____ outside his house. Xay didn't know him. The stranger _____ a beautiful new TV. The stranger _____ to sell the TV for $30. Xay said "No." He didn't buy the TV.

1. Who came home from work?

_____

2. When did he come home?

_____

3. Where was the stranger?

_____

4. What was the stranger doing?

_____

5. What did Xay say?

_____

6. Why did Xay say "No"?

_____

7. What should Xay do?

_____

HOUSING 4

Today's date _____

A. Can I help you?

B. I saw the vacancy sign. How much is the apartment?

A. It's $625 a month.

B. That's too expensive. Thanks anyway.

A. Can I help you?

B. Do you have an apartment for rent?

A. No, I don't. I can put your name on the waiting list.

B. O.K. Can I fill out the application now?

A. Sure. I'll get it.

RENTAL APPLICATION

Name: _____
           Last name   First name

Current address: _____ How long?

_____ _____
  Number Street City State Zip code

Previous address: _____ How long?

_____ _____
  Number Street City State Zip code

Married ☐   Birthdate: _____
Single ☐
Divorced ☐

How many people are going to live in the apartment? _____

Occupation _____ How long? _____

Name of company _____ ( ) _____
                                          Telephone

Address of company _____
                        Number Street City State Zip code

Monthly income $_____

Name of Bank: _____

Checking ☐ yes ☐ no Account number _____

Savings ☐ yes ☐ no Account number _____

_____ _____
          Signature   Date

Oak Park, pool
3 Bd. 2 Ba. House
children O.K.
pets O.K.

555-5432

1. How many bedrooms? _____
2. How many bathrooms? _____
3. Can children live here? _____
4. Is it a house or apartment? _____

House for rent

Big, clean, new
refrigerator, carpet
$875. 4 bd. 1-1/2 ba.
near schools

555-2468

5. How many bedrooms? _____
6. How many bathrooms? _____
7. How much is the rent? _____
8. Is it a house or apartment? _____

Denver $825
2 Bd. Apt., very clean
No Children

555-1357

9. How many bedrooms? _____
10. How many bathrooms? _____
11. Can children live here? _____
12. How much is the rent? _____

HOUSING 5

Area code _____

A. Can I see the apartment for rent?

B. Yes, you can. Let me get the key.

A. How much is the rent?

B. $700 a month.

A. Does the rent include utilities?

B. Only water.

A. Is there a security deposit?

B. Yes, there is. It's $200.

| Is there a _____ ? |

1. _____ _____ _____ cleaning deposit?

2. _____ _____ _____ rental agreement?

3. _____ _____ _____ laundry room?

4. _____ _____ _____ refrigerator?

1. Is there a garage? _____ _____ _____

2. Is there a laundry room? _____ _____ _____

3. Is there a patio? _____ _____ _____

4. Is there a table in the kitchen? _____ _____ _____

5. Is there a sofa in the bedroom? _____ _____ _____

6. Is there a TV in the bedroom? _____ _____ _____

7. Is there a barbecue on the patio? _____ _____ _____

HOUSING 6

A. I like this apartment. I want to rent it.

B. Good. You need to pay the first and last month's rent.

A. O.K. Is there a cleaning deposit too?

B. Yes, there is. It's $150.

A. When can I move in?

B. On the fifteenth. Please read the tenant rules.

1. They are moving in.

_____ _____ _____ _____.

2. They are moving out.

_____ _____ _____ _____.

Rules for Tenants

1. Don't drive or park on grass or dirt.

2. Don't waste water. Don't allow children to play with hoses.

3. Don't put trash in boxes. Put trash in plastic bags or trash cans.

4. Don't drop trash on ground. Don't litter.

5. Don't wash clothes in sink or tub. Plumbing will break.

6. Don't use barbecue inside. Charcoal is poisonous.

Yes, you can.

No, you can't.

1. Can I wash clothes in the bathtub?

   _____

2. Can I put my trash in boxes and paper bags?

   _____

3. Can I use a barbecue inside my apartment?

   _____

4. Can I park on the grass?

   _____

5. Can I play in the water?

   _____

6. Can I drop my trash on the ground?

   _____

HOUSING 7

A. What's the date?

B. It's _____ .

A. When is the rent due?

B. Every month on the first.

A. Do you keep the rent receipts?

B. Yes, I do. I keep them in a box.

```
┌──────────────────────────────────────────────────────────┐
│                              DATE  Sept. 1   NO._____     │
│  RECIEVED OF____M. Turner_____      │
│  _750. 00_____  DOLLARS      │
│  FOR _rent for September 1-30_____       │
│  PREVIOUS BALANCE  $_____                        │
│  AMOUNT PAID       $_____ _____       │
│  BALANCE DUE       $_____ BY_____       │
└──────────────────────────────────────────────────────────┘
```

1. How much is the rent? _____

2. What's the date? _____

3. Who paid? _____

4. What month is it for? _____

HOUSING 8

A. Did you pay the rent this month?

B. Oh, no! I forgot to pay it. It was due on the fifteenth.

A. Do you have to pay a late charge?

B. Yes. I think it's five dollars.

1. When is your rent due?

   _____

2. When is your telephone bill due?

   _____

3. When is your gas and electric bill due?

   _____

4. When is your water bill due?

   _____

5. When is your car payment due?

   _____

Kao had a bad experience. He went to pay his rent, but the manager was busy. The manager told him to come back later. Kao went home. The next day he went to pay his rent again. Then the manager told him the money was late. He had to pay a late charge. Kao was upset. The manager was rude.

1. Who went to pay the rent?

_____

2. Why did the manager tell Kao to come back later?

_____

3. When did Kao go to pay his rent again?

_____

4. What did the manager say to Kao the next day?

_____

5. What can Kao do next month when he pays his rent?

_____

6. Do you talk to your manager?

_____

7. Is your manager rude or polite?

_____

A. What's the matter?

B. I came home from school, and I smelled gas.

A. Did you check the pilot lights?

B. I don't know how.

A. I'm not busy right now. Let me check them.

B. Good. Thanks.

1. Do you have pilot lights in your stove? _____

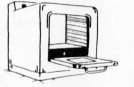

2. Do you have a pilot light in your oven? _____

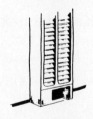

3. Do you have a pilot light in your heater? _____

4. Do you have a pilot light in your water heater? _____

HOUSING 10

Landlord's name _____

A. Can you check my electricity?

B. What's the problem?

A. The lights aren't working in my bathroom.

B. Did you pay your electric bill?

A. Yes, I did. I have my receipt.

B. I think it's a fuse. I'll come tomorrow.

In case the electricity isn't working, you need:

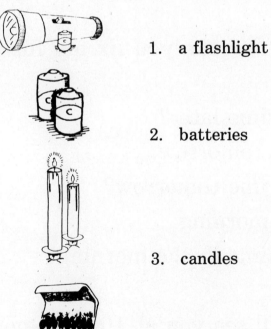

1. a flashlight

2. batteries

3. candles

4. matches

5. your manager's phone number

_____

Landlord's telephone _____

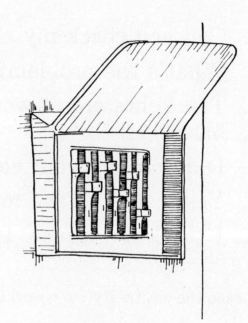

A. What time can you fix my fuse?

B. Later.

A. What time later?

B. Maybe tomorrow.

A. What time tomorrow?

B. In the morning.

A. What time in the morning?

B. 10:00.

A. O.K. I'll see you at 10:00 tomorrow morning.

Signature _____

A. Can you help me write a letter?

B. Sure. What's it about?

A. I want to move next month. I have to give my manager thirty days notice.

B. O.K. No problem, but remember to make a copy to keep.

Sept. 1, 1986

Dear Manager,

This is to inform you that we will move out in 30 days. The address is 9128 Easy Street.

Thank You.

_____

Remember the date, your name, and your address.

	Rent	Utilities	Telephone bill	Cable TV	Car insurance	Monthly total
Tom	$350	$80	$15	$13	$65	
Ann	$325	$75	$7	0	0	
You						

1. Who pays the most rent?
2. Who pays the largest phone bill?
3. Who pays the most car insurance?
4. Who pays the largest utility bill?
5. Who pays the most for cable TV?
6. What is your largest bill?
7. How much does Tom pay monthly?
8. How much does Ann pay monthly?
9. How much do you pay monthly?

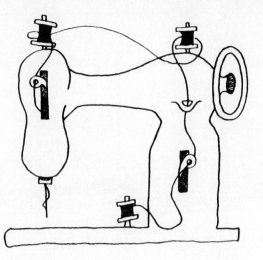

May budgets $725 a month.

Her rent is $325 a month.

Her gas and electric bill is $49.

Her telephone bill is $10.

She pays $40 a month for car gas.

She pays $250 a month for food.

She wants to buy a sewing machine for $180.

1. How much are her bills for one month?

_____

2. How much money does she have after she pays her bills?

_____

3. Can she afford to buy the sewing machine?

_____

4. How much is the sewing machine?

_____

5. How much can she save a month?

_____

6. How many months will it take to save the money for the sewing machine?

_____

1. May budgets _____ a month.

   I budget _____ .

2. Her rent is _____ a month.

   My rent is _____ .

3. Her telephone bill is _____ a month.

   My phone bill is _____ .

4. Her gas and electric bill is _____ a month.

   My gas and electric bill is _____ .

5. She pays _____ for car gas a month.

   I pay _____ for gas.

6. She can save _____ a month.

   I can save _____ .

Sept. 1, 1986

Dear Manager,

    This is to inform you that we will move out in 30 days. The address is 9128 Easy Street.

    Thank You.

_____

1. Do you have to write a _____ to your landlord before you move?

2. In case the electricity isn't working, you need a _____ and _____ .

3. If you smell gas, check your _____ _____ .

4. You can buy a used refrigerator at a _____ _____ .

5. It's important to save your _____ _____ .

6. A _____ sign means there is a place for rent.

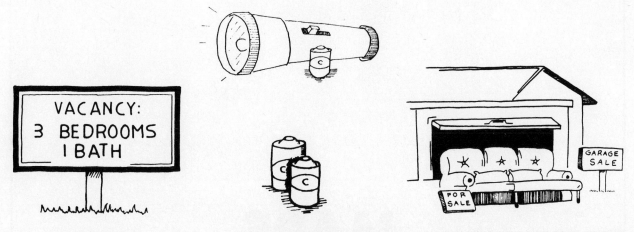

VACANCY: 3 BEDROOMS 1 BATH

GARAGE SALE

FOR SALE

6

MAPS

MAPS 1

Name _____

A. What country are you from?

B. I'm from _____ .

A. What's your native language?

B. It's _____ .

A. Can you speak any other languages?

B. Yes, I can. I speak English.

	COUNTRY	LANGUAGE
1.	France	French
2.	United States	English
3.	Mexico	Spanish
4.	China	Chinese
5.	_____	_____
6.	_____	_____
7.	_____	_____
8.	_____	_____

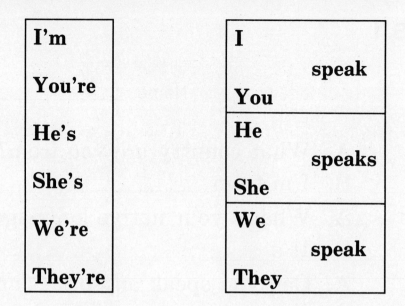

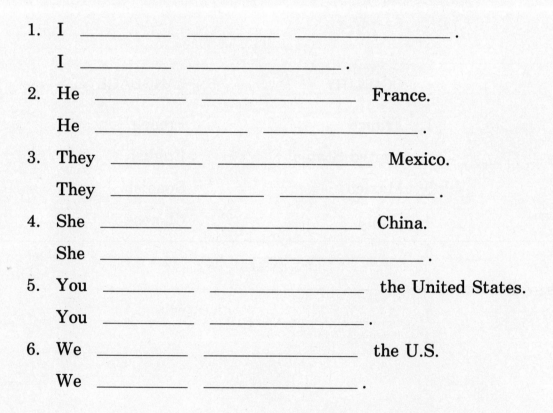

1. I _____ _____ _____.

   I _____ _____.

2. He _____ _____ France.

   He _____ _____.

3. They _____ _____ Mexico.

   They _____ _____.

4. She _____ _____ China.

   She _____ _____.

5. You _____ _____ the United States.

   You _____ _____.

6. We _____ _____ the U.S.

   We _____ _____.

North

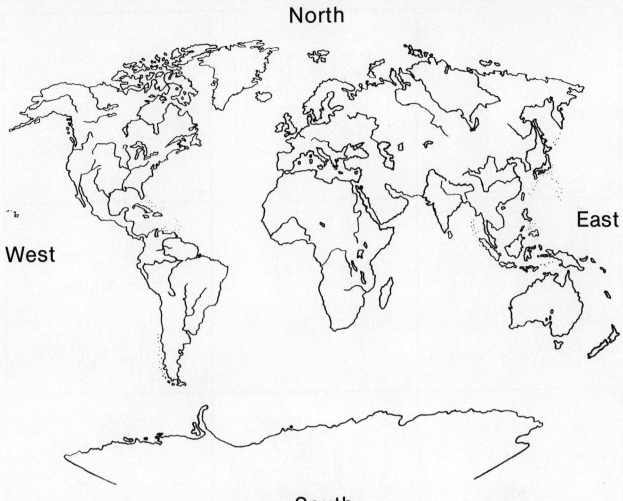

West

East

South

Color the Pacific Ocean blue.

Color the Atlantic Ocean blue.

Color the U.S. green.

Color your native country yellow.

mountains   city   hot/cold
trees   desert   rainy/dry
countryside   jungle   homesick
lake   river   ocean

MAPS 2

I speak _____ .

A. Tell me about your native country.

B. It's beautiful.

A. Did you live in | a city <br> the countryside | ?

B. _____ _____ .

A. Did you live near | a river <br> a lake <br> an ocean | ?

B. _____ _____ .

A. Are there a lot of | mountains <br> trees <br> animals <br> people <br> cars | ?

B. _____ _____ _____ .

A. Is the weather | hot <br> cold <br> rainy <br> dry | ?

B. _____ _____ _____ .

A. Are you homesick sometimes?

B. _____ _____ .

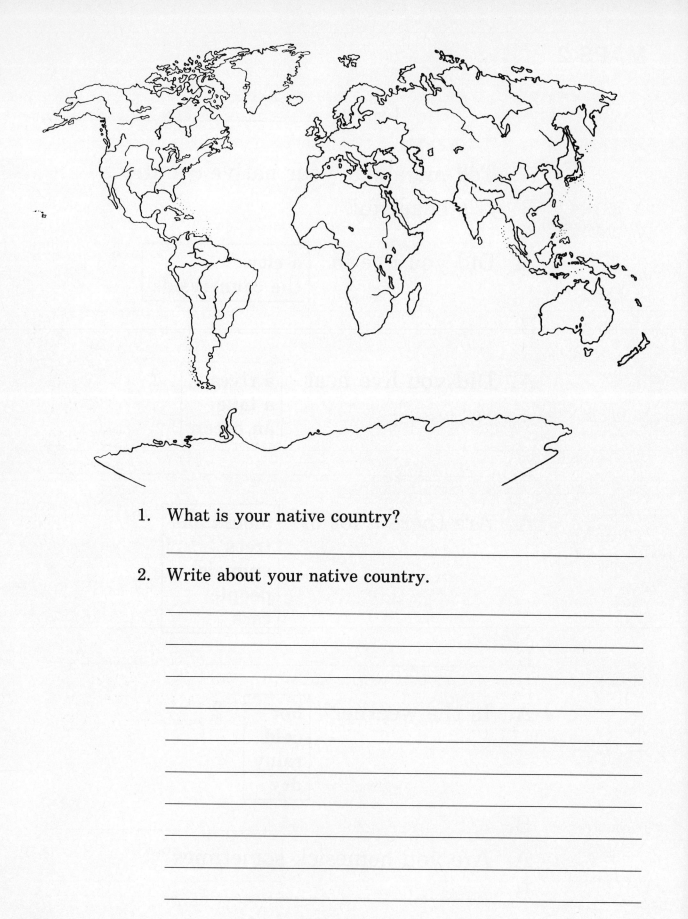

1. What is your native country?

   _____

2. Write about your native country.

   _____

   _____

   _____

   _____

   _____

   _____

   _____

   _____

   _____

   _____

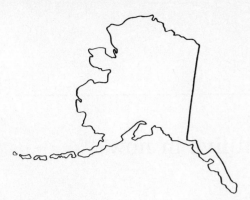

This is the United States. It has fifty states. Washington, D.C., is the capital of the United States. The President lives in Washington, D.C.

MAPS 3

My native language is _____.

    A. What country do you live in now?

    B. _____

    A. What state?

    B. _____

    A. What city?

    B. _____

    A. What's the capital of your state?

    B. _____

    A. What other states did you live in?

    B. _____

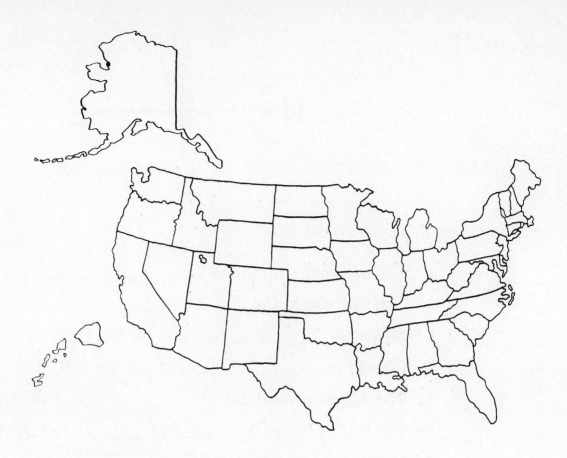

1. What country do you live in?
    Make the border green.

2. What state do you live in?
    Make it yellow.

3. What city do you live in?
    Put a red *X* on it.

4. What other states did you live in?
    Make them orange.

5. What is the capital of the U.S.?
    Put a red *X* on it.

6. Where's the Pacific Ocean?
    Make it blue.

7. Where's the Atlantic Ocean?
    Make it blue.

8. Where's Mexico?
    Make it purple.

9. Where's Canada?
    Make it pink.

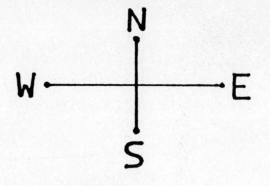

1. The sun comes up in the _____ .

2. The sun sets in the _____ .

3. Mexico is _____ of the U.S.

4. Canada is _____ of the U.S.

5. The Atlantic Ocean is _____ of the U.S.

6. The Pacific Ocean is _____ of the U.S.

7. My native country is _____ of the U.S.

My name is Hu Tran. My native country is Vietnam. My native language is Chinese. My address in the United States is 2002 South Street, Miami, Florida.

My name is Joe López. My native country is Mexico. My native language is Spanish. My address in the United States is 6879 Key Street, Yuma, Arizona.

My name is Nao Her. My native country is Laos. My native language is Hmong. My address in the United States is 3485 Tree Street, Houston, Texas.

1. What country is Hu from?

2. What country is Nao from?

3. What country is Joe from?

4. What country are you from?

5. What is Joe's native language?

6. What is Nao's native language?

7. What is your native language?

8. What is Hu's address in the U.S.?

9. What is Joe's address in the U.S.?

10. What is your address in the U.S.?

Three things I like about my new city are:

1. _____

_____ .

2. _____

_____ .

3. _____

_____ .

Three things I miss about my native country are:

1. _____

_____ .

2. _____

_____ .

3. _____

_____ .

MAPS 4

I live in _____ .

A. When did you come to the U.S.?

B. I came in 1985.

A. How did you come?

B. I flew to New York.
   Then I drove here.

A. Where did you live before?

B. I lived in   another country.
                     another state.
                     another city.
                     a refugee camp.

BEFORE	NOW
I came.	I _____ .
I flew.	I _____ .
I drove.	I _____ .
I lived.	I _____ .

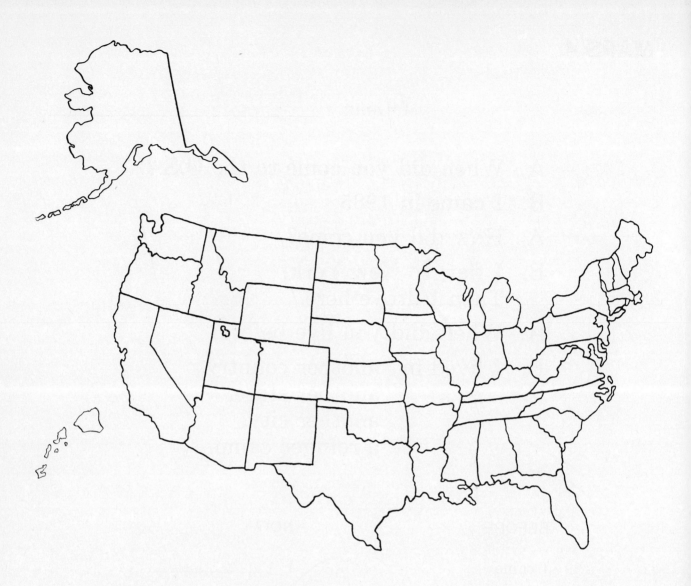

1. Did you go to New York?

2. Did you go to Alaska?

3. Did you go to Hawaii?

4. Did you go to Mexico?

5. Did you fly?

6. Did you drive?

7. Did you take a boat?

8. Did your children come with you?

9. Did your husband or wife come with you?

10. Did you arrive safely?

11. Did you cry when you left your native country?

MAPS 5

I'm from _____.

A. How did you come to the U.S.A.?

B. First I _____ to _____.

Then I _____

_____

_____.

How about you?

1. I drove.

2. I walked.

3. I flew.

4. I took a boat.

	Born	Married	First child	Left native country	Came to the U.S.	Began school
Juan	1955	1978	1982	1983	1983	1986
May	1949	1965	1967	1980	1982	1984
My friend						

was born
had a baby
came

got married
came
started

had	got married	came
came	was born	started

Anna _____ in Poland in 1951. She

_____ in 1971. She _____ her

first child in 1974. Her husband _____ to the

United States in 1976. She _____ to the U.S.

with their child in 1984. She _____ school in

1987. She wants to become a citizen. She's learning the Pledge

of Allegiance now.

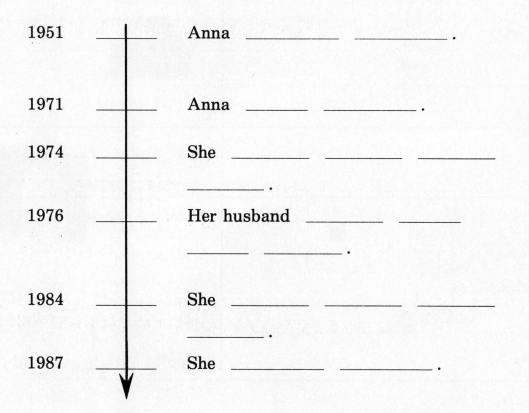

1951 _____ Anna _____ _____ .

1971 _____ Anna _____ _____ .

1974 _____ She _____ _____ _____

_____ .

1976 _____ Her husband _____ _____

_____ _____ .

1984 _____ She _____ _____ _____

_____ .

1987 _____ She _____ _____ .

I was born in _____ in _____ .

I got married in _____ . I had my first child in

_____ . I came to the U.S. in _____ .

I started school in _____ .

DATE   WHAT HAPPENED?

_____   I was born.

153

I pledge allegiance to the flag of the United States of America and to the republic for which it stands, one nation, under God, indivisible, with liberty and justice for all.

This is the flag of the United States. It's red, white, and blue. It has thirteen stripes and fifty stars. There is one stripe for each of the first thirteen states. There is one star for each of the fifty states.

1. This is the flag of _____ _____
_____ . It's red, white, and blue. It has
thirteen _____ and fifty _____
on it.

2. This is the flag of my native country, _____ .
It's _____ .

1. I'm living in the U.S., and I'm studying _____ in school now.

2. The _____ of the U.S. has fifty stars and thirteen stripes.

3. The President of the U.S. lives in _____ .

4. I live in _____ .

5. My native country is _____ .

6. My native language is _____ .

7

TRANSPORTATION

TRANSPORTATION 1

Name _____

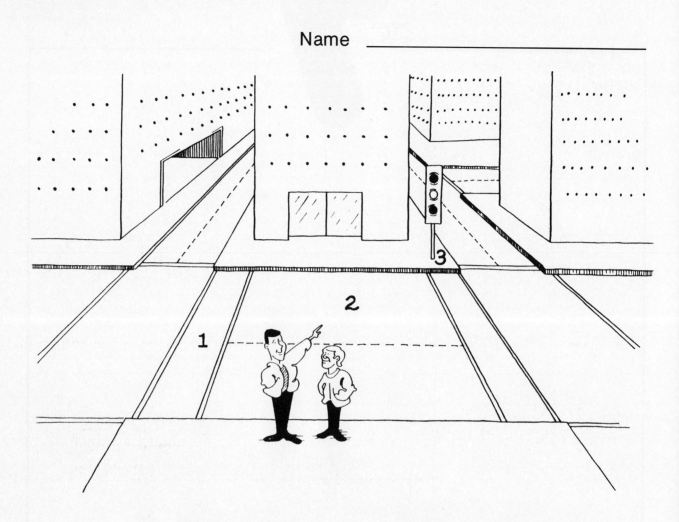

A. Don't cross in the middle of the street.

B. Why not?

A. It's illegal. You can get a ticket. Cross at the corner or at the light.

B. O.K. Let's cross now. The light says walk.

Number 1 is a _____ .

Number 2 is the _____ _____ _____ .

Number 3 is a _____ or _____ .

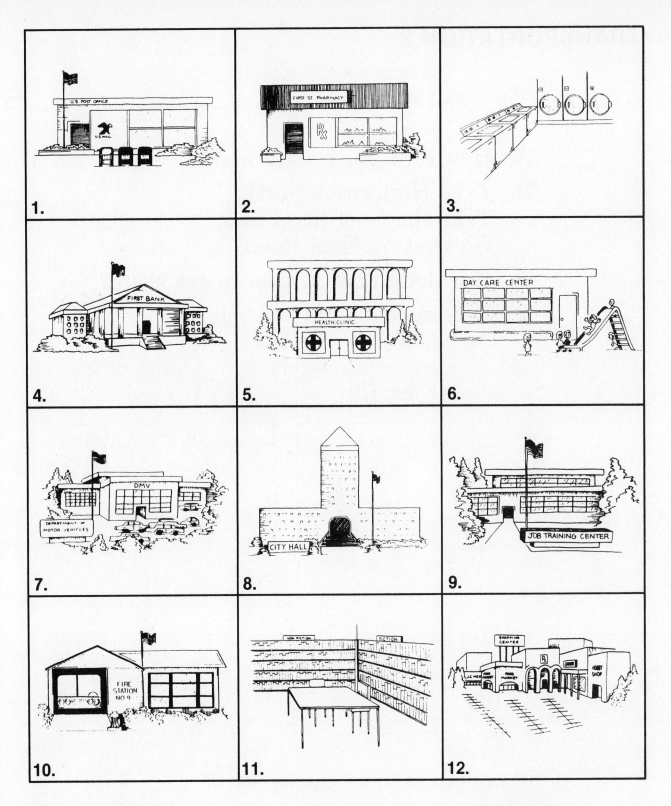

post office pharmacy laundromat
bank   clinic   day-care center
D.M.V.   city hall job training center
fire station library   shopping center

TRANSPORTATION 2

Social security no. _____

A. How do I get to city hall?

B. Take Highway 5 north.
Take the Noel Road exit.
Go west on Noel Road.

A. How long does it take to get there?

B. It takes about fifteen minutes.

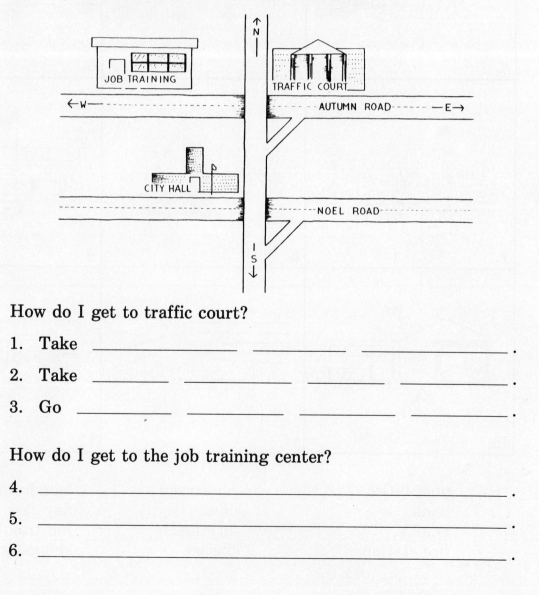

How do I get to traffic court?

1. Take _____ _____ _____ .

2. Take _____ _____ _____ .

3. Go _____ _____ _____ _____ .

How do I get to the job training center?

4. _____ .

5. _____ .

6. _____ .

1. How long does it take to get to the post office?

   It takes about _____ minutes.

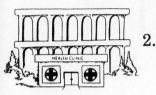

2. How long does it take to get to the clinic?

   It takes about _____ _____.

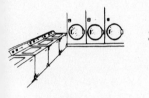

3. How long does it take to get to the laundromat?

   It takes _____ _____ _____.

4. How long does it take to get to the pharmacy?

   It _____ _____ _____ _____.

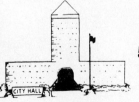

5. How long does it take to get to city hall?

   _____ _____ _____ _____.

6. How long does it take to get to the D.M.V.?

   _____ _____ _____ _____.

TRANSPORTATION 3

Age _____

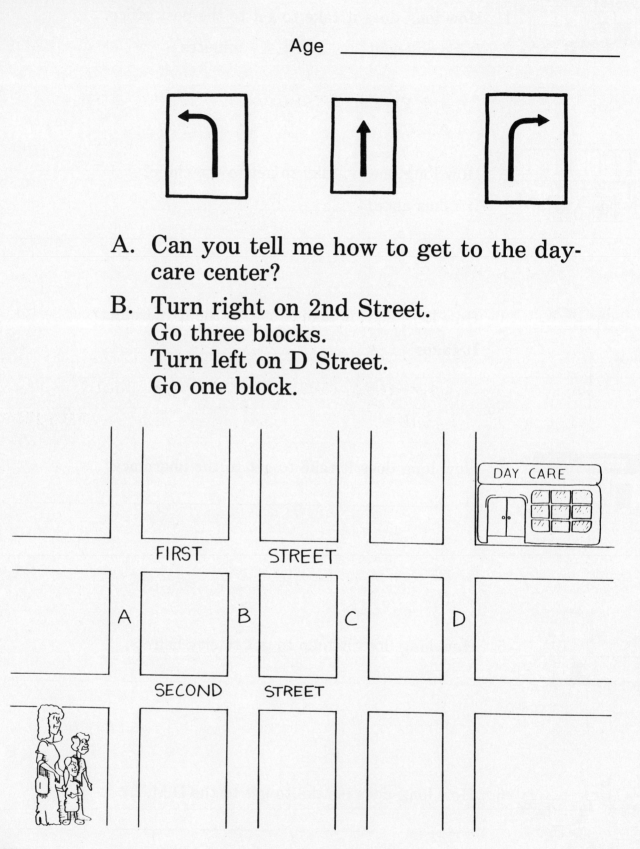

A. Can you tell me how to get to the day-care center?

B. Turn right on 2nd Street.
Go three blocks.
Turn left on D Street.
Go one block.

TRANSPORTATION 4

City _____

    A. Can you give me directions to your
       house?

    B. Sure. Go to _____

_____

_____

_____

_____.

    A. What's the address?

    B. It's _____.

    A. How long does it take to get there?

    B. It takes about _____ minutes.

Al usually walks to school. It takes about twenty minutes. Yesterday he took the bus. He wants to buy a car soon. Then he will drive.

Yesterday	Usually	Later
walked		will walk
	take takes	will take
drove	drive drives	

1. Does he usually take the bus to school?

   _____

2. Does he usually walk to school?

   _____

3. Did he take the bus to school yesterday?

   _____

4. Will he buy a car soon?

   _____

	Yesterday	Usually	Tomorrow
	She _____ a car to school.	She _____ a bus to school.	She _____ to school.
	He _____ to school.	He _____ a car home.	He _____ a bus to New York.
	They _____ a bus to Los Angeles.	They _____ to school.	They _____ a car to New York.

TRANSPORTATION 5

State _____

GATES 5-9
PAL AIRLINES
SNACK BAR

GATES 10-15
LUGGAGE CLAIM
RESTROOMS

A. Can you tell me where PAL Airlines is?

B. Go straight to the telephones, and turn left.

A. Oh, I see the sign now. Thanks.

1. _____

2. _____

3. _____

TRANSPORTATION 6

Country _____

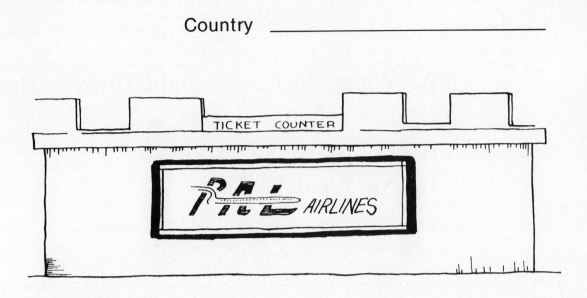

A. Here's my ticket.

B. Do you have any luggage?

A. Yes, I do.

B. Let's check it in. What about that box?

A. I'm going to carry it on.

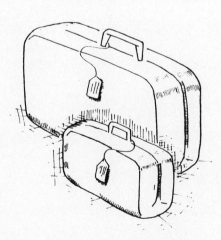 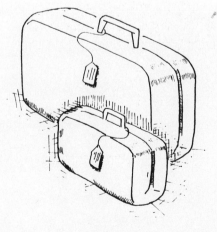

1. _____ or _____

TRANSPORTATION 7

Zip _____

A. Where do I meet flight 10 from Hawaii?
B. It's arriving at gate 7.
A. Is it on time?
B. No, it's delayed.

Flight number	Arriving from	Time	
789	Dallas	7:16 P.M.	on time
20	New York	10:00 A.M.	on time
10	Hawaii	2:30	delayed
5	Mexico City	8:05	on time

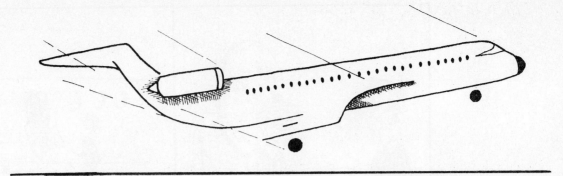

1. Flight 10 should arrive at 2:30.

   It's one hour late. What time will it arrive? _____

2. Flight 21 should arrive at 12:30.

   It's three hours late. What time will it arrive? _____

3. Flight 57 should arrive at 4:00.

   It's one and a half hours late. What time will it arrive? ___

4. Flight 14 should arrive at 10:00.

   It's twenty-five minutes late. What time will it arrive? ___

5. Flight 99 should arrive at 7:45.

   It's thirty minutes late. What time will it arrive? _____

6. Flight 38 should arrive at 8:45.

   It's on time. What time will it arrive? _____

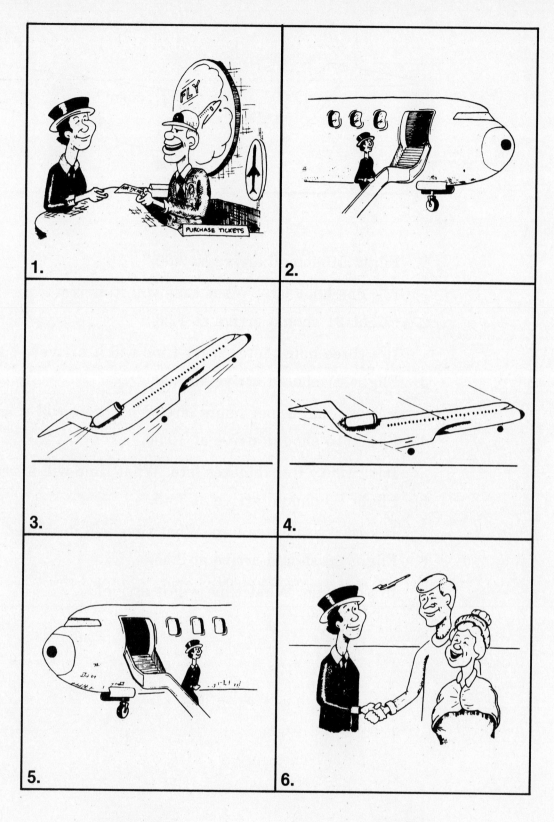

checked in
took off
got

boarded
landed
met

boarded	took off	landed
checked in	met	got

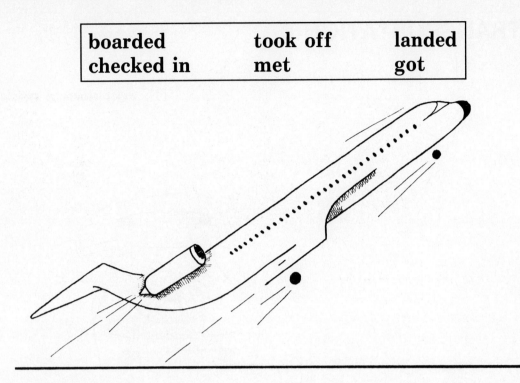

Bob went to the airport to take a plane to New York. He wanted to find a job. He _____ _____ at the ticket counter. His plane was leaving, so he _____ at gate 15. He sat down and put on his seat belt. The plane _____ _____ for New York. He _____ in New York. He _____ his luggage and _____ his friends. Good luck, Bob!

1. Where did Bob take a plane?
2. Where did he check in?
3. Why did Bob want to go to New York?
4. Who met Bob at the airport?
5. At what gate did Bob board?
6. Did you ever take a plane?
7. Where did you go?

TRANSPORTATION 8

Do you own a car? yes ☐

no ☐

A. Hello.

B. Hello. I'm calling about the car for sale.

A. Yes.

B. How much is it?

A. It's $1800.

B. What year?

A. '84.

B. What make?

A. Chevrolet.

B. How many miles does it have?

A. 90,000.

B. How are the tires?

A. They're O.K.

| Car for Sale |
| runs good |
| call 555-3192 |

Chevy Van '79
new tires
$4,000   automatic
555-1589

1. What year is it? _____
2. What make is it?

_____

'82   Honda
air   5 speed
Xlnt condition
555-1035

3. What year is it? _____
4. What make is it?

_____

Ford Wagon
'71   runs O.K.
rebuilt engine
$700   555-7798

5. What year is it? _____
6. What make is it?

_____

Toyota Sedan '87
good condition
4 door   4 speed
air   555-7281

7. What year is it? _____
8. What make is it?

_____

TRANSPORTATION 9

Do you have a car? yes ☐

no ☐

A. What condition is the car in?

B. It's in good condition.

A. Can I come and see it this afternoon?

B. Yes. I'll be home after 2:00.

A. O.K. I'll come at 3:00. Can I take it for a test drive?

B. O.K.

1. _____

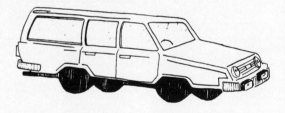

2. _____

3. _____

4. _____

Chevrolet	Toyota	Ford
Station wagon	Pickup truck	Van
1974	1982	1977
$3,000	$4,500	$2,500
90,000	17,000	36,000

1. Which one is the cheapest?
2. Which one is the most expensive?
3. Which one is the newest?
4. Which one is the oldest?
5. Which one has the most miles?
6. Which one has the least miles?
7. Which one do you want to buy?

What make is your car? _____

A. How much do you want for your car?

B. I want $1800.

A. Will you take $1500?

B. I'll take $1700.

A. $1650?

B. O.K.

A. Will you take a check?

B. No, I won't. Cash only.

JOE DOE   101
123 FIRST AVE.
U.S. AMERICA 10011   DATE _____

PAY TO THE ORDER OF _____

_____ DOLLARS

JG BANK   _____
                           SIGNATURE

1. Will he take a check?

   _____

2. Will he take cash?

   _____

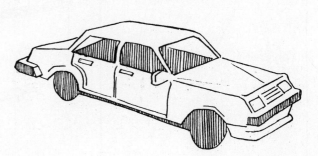

1. How much _____ you _____ for your car?

2. How much _____ he _____ for his van?

3. How much _____ they _____ for their pickup truck?

4. How much _____ she _____ for her station wagon?

5. How much _____ he _____ for _____ truck?

6. How much _____ you _____ for _____ station wagon?

7. How much _____ she _____ for _____ van?

8. How much _____ they _____ for _____ car?

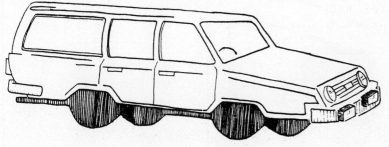

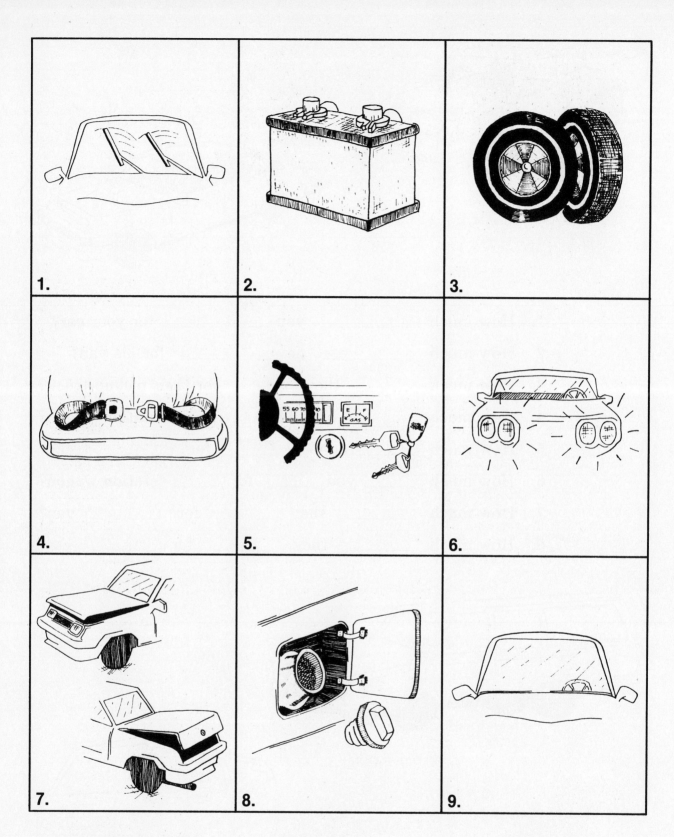

1.

2.

3.

4.

5.

6.

7.

8.

9.

windshield wipers battery   tires
seat belts   ignition/key   headlights
hood/trunk   gas tank/cap   windshield

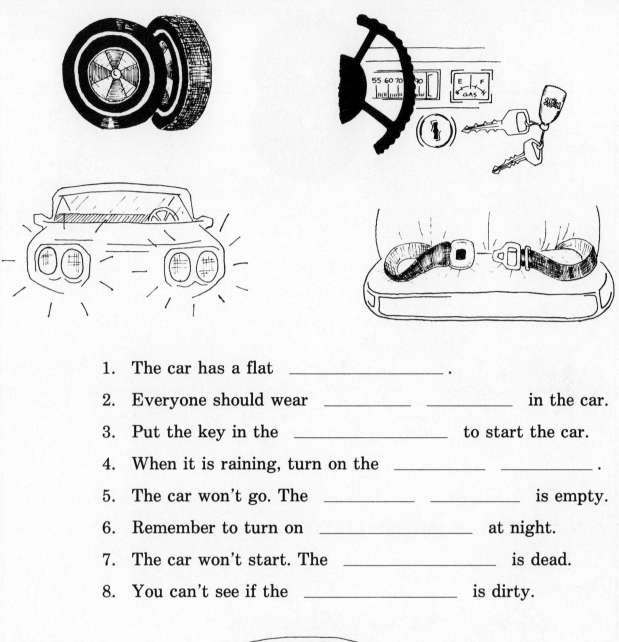

1. The car has a flat _____.

2. Everyone should wear _____ _____ in the car.

3. Put the key in the _____ to start the car.

4. When it is raining, turn on the _____ _____.

5. The car won't go. The _____ _____ is empty.

6. Remember to turn on _____ at night.

7. The car won't start. The _____ is dead.

8. You can't see if the _____ is dirty.

8

EMERGENCIES

EMERGENCIES 1

Emergency police number _____

A. Did you hear about the earthquake?

B. Yes, I did. It was terrible.

A. The newspaper says there will always be earthquakes.

B. That's bad news.

A. But there is good news. Every day scientists are learning more about earthquakes.

1. _____

3. _____

2. _____

4. _____

DAILY PAPER
TWENTY-FIVE CENTS
FINAL EDITION

DAILY PAPER
25¢
SEPTEMBER 12 1987

TIMES

· FINAL EDITION ·
· FINAL EDITION ·

GOOD NEWS	BAD NEWS
1.	1.
	2.
2.	3.
3.	4.

Big Earthquake in Mexico

Missing Boy Comes Home

Car Accident Hurts Three

Police Get Purse Snatcher

Hurricane Comes to Florida

Bad Storm over Mountains

In case of emergencies, you should have these in your home:

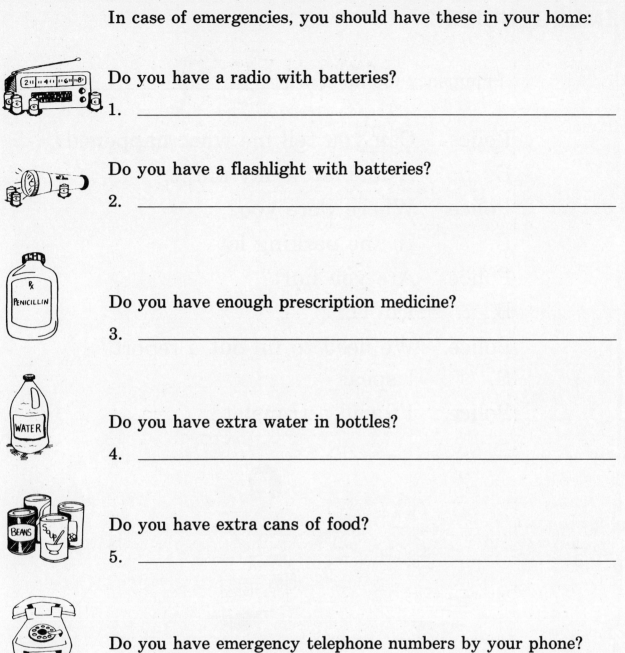

Do you have a radio with batteries?

1. _____

Do you have a flashlight with batteries?

2. _____

Do you have enough prescription medicine?

3. _____

Do you have extra water in bottles?

4. _____

Do you have extra cans of food?

5. _____

Do you have emergency telephone numbers by your phone?

6. _____

EMERGENCIES 2

Emergency fire number _____

Police.   Can you tell me what happened?

B.   A man stole my purse.

Police.   Where were you?

B.   In the parking lot.

Police.   Are you hurt?

B.   I'm O.K.

Police.   We need to fill out a report.

B.   I speak _____ .

Police.   I'll call a translator.

EMERGENCIES 3

Non-emergency police number _____

A. I'm calling to report that somebody robbed my house. My TV is missing.

B. Is there someone in the house now?

A. No.

B. What else is missing?

A. I don't know. I have to check.

B. Don't touch anything. The police will come soon.

1. What's the non-emergency police number in your area?

   _____

2. What's the emergency police number in your area?

   _____

3. Do you have the numbers next to your telephone?

   _____

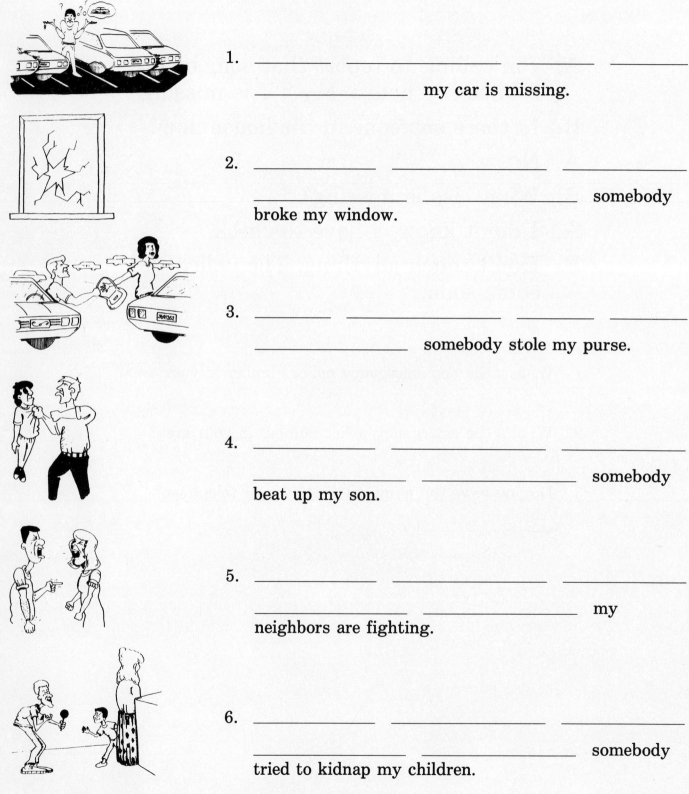

1. _____ _____ _____
   _____ my car is missing.

2. _____ _____ _____
   _____ _____ somebody
   broke my window.

3. _____ _____ _____
   _____ somebody stole my purse.

4. _____ _____ _____
   _____ _____ somebody
   beat up my son.

5. _____ _____ _____
   _____ _____ my
   neighbors are fighting.

6. _____ _____ _____
   _____ _____ somebody
   tried to kidnap my children.

I You We They	have to
He She	has to

1. My car is missing. I _____ _____ call the police.

2. Somebody stole her purse. She _____ _____ call the police.

3. Somebody beat up our son. We _____ _____ take him to the doctor.

4. Somebody broke his window. He _____ _____ call his landlord.

5. My neighbors are fighting. I _____ _____ call the police.

6. Their children said a man was watching them. They

_____ _____ call the police.

EMERGENCIES 4

Non-emergency fire number _____

A. Let's fill out this police report.

B. O.K.

A. What's missing?

B. My color TV.

A. What brand?

B. I don't remember.

A. What color?

B. Brown.

A. How much did it cost?

B. About $200.

What's missing?	What brand?	What color?	How much did it cost?
color TV	Sears	brown	$200

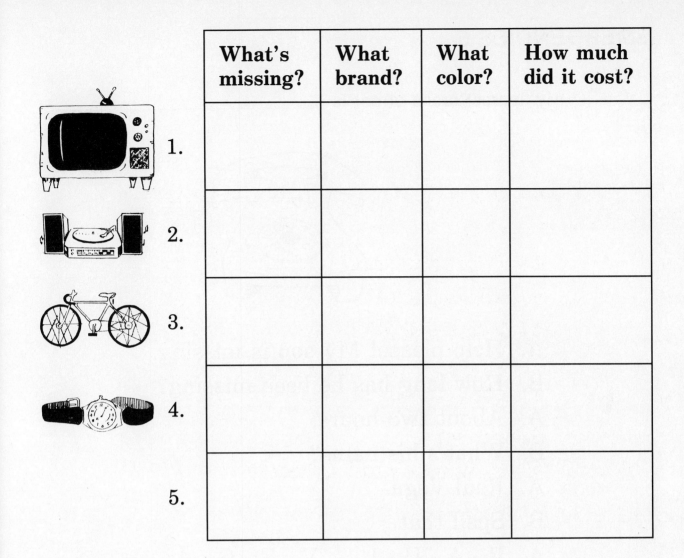

	What's missing?	What brand?	What color?	How much did it cost?
1.				
2.				
3.				
4.				
5.				

EMERGENCIES 5

My nearest cross street is _____ .

A. Help please! My son is missing.

B. How long has he been missing?

A. About two hours.

B. What's his name?

A. Raul Vega.

B. Spell that.

A. R - A - U - L   V - E - G - A.

B. Does he speak English?

A. Yes, he does.

B. Stay calm. Don't leave your house. A police officer will come soon.

EMERGENCIES 6

Health clinic number _____

A. What does he look like?

B. He's about four feet tall. He's thin. He has curly black hair. He has brown eyes.

A. What was he wearing?

B. He was wearing blue jeans, a brown sweater, and white tennis shoes.

A. How old is he?

B. He's seven years old.

A. Did you talk to his friends?

B. Yes, I did. He's not with his friends.

What does he / she look like?

_____ fat.

_____ short.

_____ curly hair.

1. _____ dark hair.

_____ tall.

_____ thin.

_____ short hair

2. _____ old.

_____ short.

_____ thin.

_____ blue eyes.

3. _____ brown hair.

_____ young.

_____ little.

_____ long hair.

4. _____ brown eyes.

1. What was he wearing?

   _____ _____ _____

   jeans, a dark sweater, and white tennis shoes.

2. What was she wearing?

   _____ _____ _____

   a skirt, sandals, and a jacket.

3. What are you wearing?

   _____

   _____

   _____

4. What's your teacher wearing?

   _____

   _____

   _____

Do you have car insurance? yes ☐
no ☐

A. _____ can't come to school today.

B. Why? What happened?

A. He was in a car accident.

B. Oh no! How is he?

A. He has a broken leg.

B. Was he wearing a seat belt?

A. Yes, he was.

B. Does he have insurance?

A. Yes, he does. But it wasn't his fault.

1.  He was hit from behind.
He was rear-ended.

2.  He was hit head on.

EMERGENCIES 8

Hospital emergency room _____

A. Oh no. That car hit the little boy.

B. It's a hit-and-run. Get the license number.

A. O.K. I'll call the police too. You help the boy.

1. What's the license plate number?

_____

2. What's the license plate number?

_____

1. Don't leave the injured person.

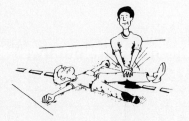

2. Cover the person with a jacket or blanket.

3. Stop bleeding with pressure.

4. Stay calm. Get help. Tell the person that help is coming.

What's the telephone number?

1. Emergency police _____

2. Emergency fire _____

3. Emergency accident _____

4. Poison control center _____

5. Non-emergency police _____

6. Non-emergency fire _____

7. Hospital emergency room _____

8. Gas and electric emergency turn-off _____

9. Food stamp office _____

10. Health clinic _____

11. My doctor _____

12. My school _____

13. My landlord _____

14. My friend _____

EMERGENCIES 9

Poison control center number _____

A. Poison control center.

B. My daughter ate some aspirin.

A. How old is she?

B. Two and a half.

A. How much does she weigh?

B. About thirty pounds.

A. How many did she take?

B. Ten or twelve.

A. What time did this happen?

B. Fifteen minutes ago.

A. Is she conscious?

B. Yes, she is.

A. Take her to the nearest emergency room.

1. He's _____ .   2. He's _____ .

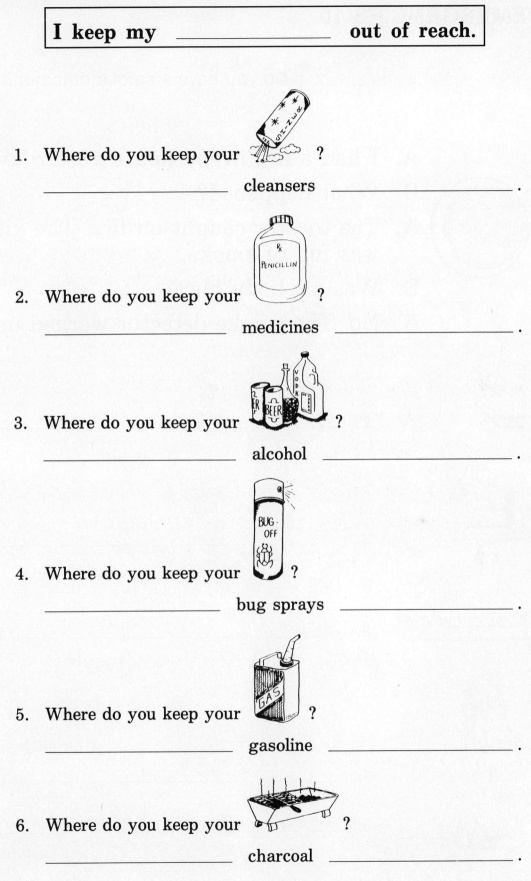

| I keep my _____ out of reach. |

1. Where do you keep your ?

    _____ cleansers _____ .

2. Where do you keep your ?

    _____ medicines _____ .

3. Where do you keep your ?

    _____ alcohol _____ .

4. Where do you keep your ?

    _____ bug sprays _____ .

5. Where do you keep your ?

    _____ gasoline _____ .

6. Where do you keep your ?

    _____ charcoal _____ .

EMERGENCIES 10

Do you have a smoke detector?   yes ☐

no ☐

A. I had a fire in my house yesterday.

B. What happened?

A. The toaster caught on fire. The kitchen was full of smoke.

B. Was anybody hurt?

A. No. The smoke detector warned us early.

1. _____ .

2. _____ .

3. _____ .

4. _____ .

5. _____

_____ .

Last night somebody climbed upstairs and came in Pat's window. Pat's daughter saw the man. The man had long dark hair. He was wearing jeans, a sweatshirt, and tennis shoes. He stole about fifteen records and cassettes. Pat was very afraid, but she didn't call the police. She was too afraid to sleep. The next day she was afraid to leave her house.

1. How did the thief get into Pat's house?
2. What did he steal?
3. Who saw him?
4. What was he wearing?
5. What did he look like?
6. When was Pat's house robbed?
7. Did Pat call the police?
8. Was Pat afraid?

She should

Next time what should Pat do?

1. _____ _____ call the police.

2. _____ _____ lock the windows.

3. _____ _____ tell her landlord. ما يقول كلمات

4. _____ _____ warn her neighbors.

5. _____ _____ _____

_____ .

6. If there is someone in my house, I should _____

_____

_____

_____ .

SIGNS

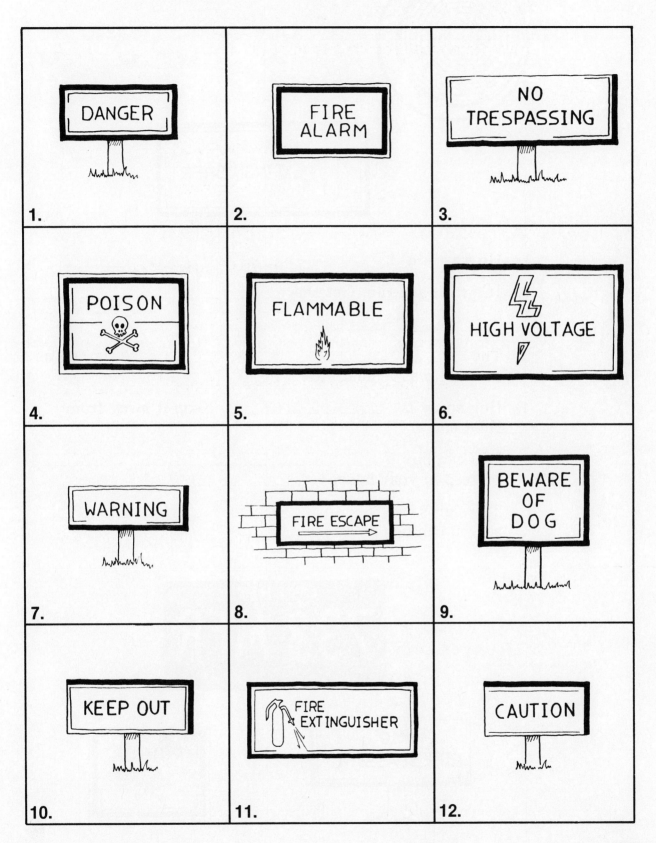

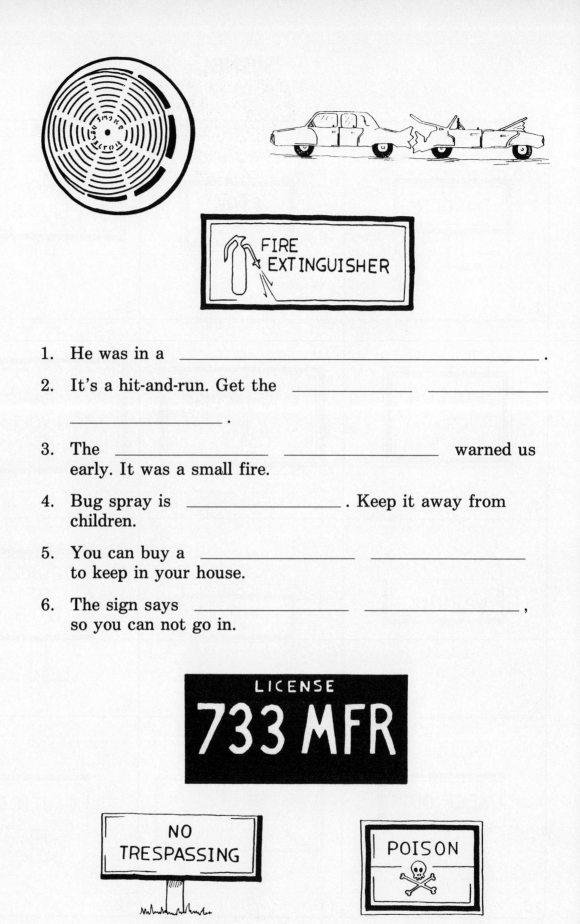

1. He was in a _____ .

2. It's a hit-and-run. Get the _____ _____

   _____ .

3. The _____ _____ warned us
   early. It was a small fire.

4. Bug spray is _____ . Keep it away from
   children.

5. You can buy a _____ _____
   to keep in your house.

6. The sign says _____ _____ ,
   so you can not go in.

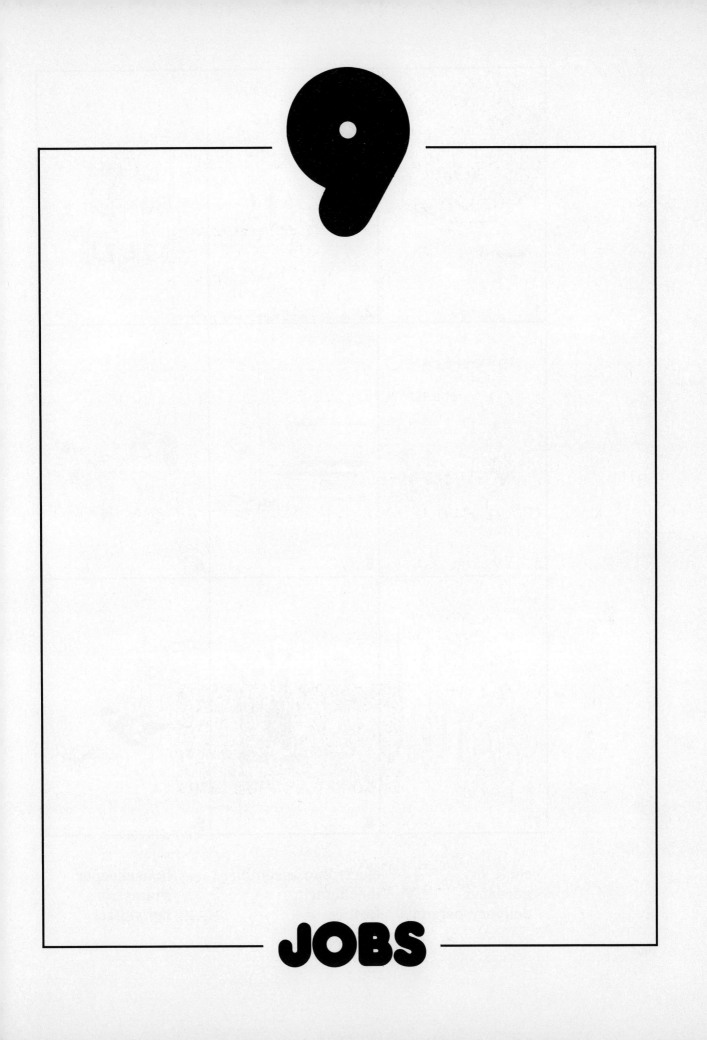

JOBS

cook
gardener
delivery person

electronic assembler
mechanic
farmer

housekeeper
seamstress
babysitter

JOBS 1

Today's date _____

A. Is Tekaa here today?

B. No, she isn't. She has a part-time job.

A. Really?

B. Yes. She's | **babysitting.**
cleaning houses.
mowing lawns.
delivering newspapers. |

1. _____

3. _____

2. _____

4. _____

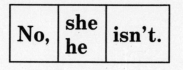

1. Is he babysitting?

   No, _____ _____ .

   He's _____ _____ .

2. Is she delivering newspapers?

   No, _____ _____ .

   She's _____ _____ .

3. Is she babysitting?

   No, _____ _____ .

   She's _____ _____ .

4. Is she mowing lawns?

   No, _____ _____ .

   She's _____ _____ .

JOBS 2

A. I can't come to the school anymore.

B. I'm sorry. Why not?

A. My husband got a full-time job. Nobody can take care of my baby.

B. What about your sister?

A. She wants to get a part-time job.

B. We'll miss you.

1. Does your | **husband** **wife** | have a job?

    _____ .

2. Does your sister have a job?

    _____ .

3. Do you have a full-time job?

    _____ .

4. Do you have a part-time job?

    _____ .

JOBS 3

Social security number _____

A. My friend is looking for a part-time job.

B. There's a sign in the window at McJack's.

A. What should she do?

B. She should go inside and ask for an application.

1.

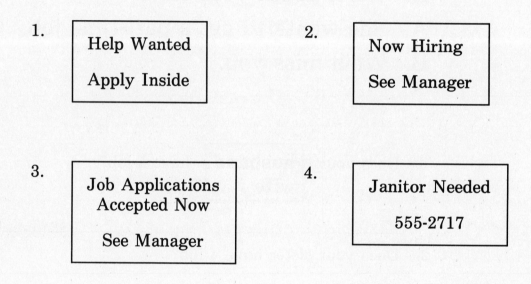

Help Wanted

Apply Inside

2.

Now Hiring

See Manager

3.

Job Applications
Accepted Now

See Manager

4.

Janitor Needed

555-2717

JOBS 4

Birthplace _____

```
┌─────────────────┐
│   Cook Wanted   │
│  No experience  │
│    Part-time    │
│    555-3284     │
└─────────────────┘
```

A. Can I help you?

B. I want to ask about your ad for a cook.

A. Sure.

B. How much does it pay?

A. Starting pay is $5.50 an hour.

B. Are there benefits?

A. We have health insurance.

B. Could I have an application please?

A. Here it is.

B. Thank you.

JOB APPLICATION

Name: _____
               Last name   First name

Address: _____
          Number   Street   City

_____ (   )_____
   State   Zip code   Telephone

_____ _____-_____-_____
   Date of birth   Social security number

Birthplace:

Education: What schools have you attended?

Elementary school   yes ☐

                         no ☐

High school   yes ☐

                         no ☐

College   yes ☐

                         no ☐

Job training program   yes ☐

                         no ☐

Job experience   yes ☐

                         no ☐

What was your job? _____ How long? _____

Signature _____ Date _____

JOBS 5

Date of birth _____

> Wanted:
> Gardeners
> with experience
> 555-0871

A. Hello.

B. Hello. I want to apply for the gardener job.

A. Do you have experience?

B. Yes, I do. I was a farmer for ten years.

A. You'll have to talk to the boss. Call back tomorrow at 10 A.M.

B. O.K. Thank you.

Babysitter needed No experience 555-0821 1.	1. What is the job? _____ . 2. Do you need experience? _____ .
Wanted: Mechanic 2 yrs. experience 555-2141 2.	3. What is the job? _____ . 4. Do you need experience? _____ .
Electronic Assemblers needed 1 yr. experience 3.	5. What is the job? _____ . 6. Do you need experience? _____ .
Wanted: Housekeeper No experience 555-3827 4.	7. What is the job? _____ . 8. Do you need experience? _____ .
Men and Women wanted to deliver newspapers No experience 5.	9. What is the job? _____ . 10. Do you need experience? _____ .

Villa is looking for a part-time job. She's a student now. She studies English every day. She wants to be a nurse. She was a nurse in Iran. She has two years experience.

1. Who is looking for a job?

_____

2. What is she now?

_____

3. What does she study every day?

_____

4. What does she want to be?

_____

5. What was her job in Iran?

_____

6. How many years experience does she have?

_____

7. What was your job in your country?

_____

8. How many years experience do you have?

_____

Villa Mahmet wants to apply for a job. Her address is 1676 Fulton Street, Santa Ana, California. Her zip code is 92701. Her telephone number is 555-2000. Her date of birth is June 6, 1957. Her social security number is 007-32-8114.

JOB APPLICATION

Name: _____

        Last name   First name

Address: _____

       Number   Street   City

_____

  State   Zip code   Telephone

_____

  Date of birth   Social security number

Villa is from Iran. She went to school in her country. She went to elementary school, high school, and college. She was a nurse for two years. She has job experience. She has two years job experience as a nurse.

Birthplace:

Education: What schools have you attended?

Elementary school   yes ☐

                                  no ☐

High school   yes ☐

                                  no ☐

College   yes ☐

                                  no ☐

Job training program   yes ☐

                                  no ☐

Job experience   yes ☐

                                  no ☐

What was your job? _____ How long? _____

Signature _____ Date _____

Job experience   yes ☐
                 no ☐

A. I have to go home early today.

B. Why?

A. I have an appointment at the job training center.

B. What for?

A. I have to talk to my job counselor. I want to enroll in

| electronic assembly. |
| machine shop. |
| auto repair. |
| power sewing. |

1. Do you have a job training center in your area?

    _____

2. What's the address of the job training center?

    _____

3. Do you have a job counselor?

    _____

4. What's your job counselor's name?

    _____

5. What do you want to enroll in?

    _____

JOBS 7

Social security number _____

A. I'm happy to tell you, you have the job.

B. Thanks. When do I start?

A. Be here tomorrow at 9:00 to fill out your insurance and tax forms. You can start next week.

B. I'll be here. Thanks.

Remember to:

1. shake hands
2. smile
3. be on time.

JOBS 8

A. Pang got a job.

B. That's great! What days does she work?

A. Monday, Wednesday, and Saturday.

B. What are her hours?

A. From 4 P.M. to 9 P.M.
   She works the night shift.

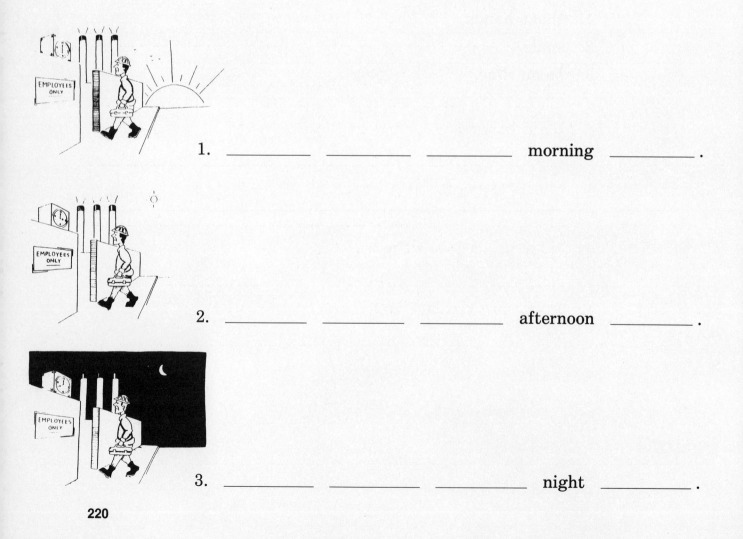

1. _____ _____ _____ morning _____.

2. _____ _____ _____ afternoon _____.

3. _____ _____ _____ night _____.

220

The Night Shift Schedule

	M	T	W	Th	F	Sat.	Sun.
Pang	4-9		4-9			4-9	
Lin		4-9		4-9			
Tom				5-9	5-9		5-9

1. What days does Lin work?

   _____

2. What hours does Lin work?

   _____

3. What days does Tom work?

   _____

4. What hours does Tom work?

   _____

5. What days does Pang work?

   _____

6. What hours does Pang work?

   _____

7. What shift do they work?

   _____

JOBS 9

I attended high school.   yes ☐
                            no ☐

A. I think there's a mistake on my paycheck.

B. Do you have your stub?

A. Yes, here it is. But I don't understand it.

B. Let's look at it.

BIG CO.

FEB. 10, 1988

PAY TO
ORDER OF___KAO VUE___ $157.50

ONE HUNDRED FIFTY SEVEN 50/100   DOLLARS

MR. NORTH, PRESIDENT

1. The part of the paycheck you keep is the _____.

2. The part of the paycheck you cash is the _____.

NAME: KAO VUE		
HOURS	GROSS PAY	NET PAY
35	$ 183.75	$ 157.50
F. I. C. A	FEDERAL TAX	STATE TAX
$ 5.25	$ 18.40	$ 2.60

Match

1. stub   total hours you work

2. hours   Social Security

3. gross pay   the money you take home

4. net pay   the money the state takes

5. F.I.C.A.   all the money you make

6. federal tax   the part of the paycheck you keep

7. state tax   the money the U.S. government takes

NAME: KAO VUE		
HOURS	GROSS PAY	NET PAY
35	$ 183.75	$ 157. 50
F.I.C.A	FEDERAL TAX	STATE TAX
$ 5.25	$ 18.40	$ 2.60

1. What is the name on the stub?

   _____

2. What are the total hours worked?

   _____

3. What is the net pay?

   _____

4. What is the gross pay?

   _____

5. How much does he pay to Social Security?

   _____

6. How much does he pay to the state?

   _____

7. How much does he pay to the U.S. government?

   _____

JOBS 10

What was your job in your country? _____

A. What's this pink paper with my paycheck?

B. I'm sorry. You got laid off.

A. Why?

B. Because there isn't enough work for everyone.

A. When can I work again?

B. I'm not sure. I'll call you when there's more work.

Match

1. hired   not enough work
2. laid off   get a job
3. fired   lose job

Native country _____

A. In my native country, I was a farmer.

B. What did you do each day?

A. I worked very hard. I grew corn, cucumbers, and rice.

B. Did you take care of animals too?

A. Yes, I did. I had some chickens and pigs. I never went to the grocery store.

B. Life was different there.

A. Yes. Life is very different here too.

1. Are you working now?

   _____

2. Did you work in your country?

   _____

3. What was your job?

   _____

4. Was your job easy?

   _____

5. Was your job difficult?

   _____

6. Did you like your job?

   _____

7. Do you want a job in the U.S.?

   _____

8. What job do you want?

   _____

9. How many years of job experience do you have?

   _____

In my native country, Peru, I was a baker. It was difficult work. I worked every day from 4:00 in the morning to 6:00 at night. I did a good job. People liked to eat the cookies and bolillos from the bakery.

In my native country, _____ , I was a

_____ . It was _____ work. I

worked from _____ in the morning to

_____ . I did a _____ job.

Din had a job in an office building. He was a janitor on the night shift. He was in charge of many things. He was in charge of cleaning some offices.

He did a good job. Everyone liked him. Then one night his boss gave him a raise. He gave him the keys to the building too.

Din was very proud. Now he was in charge of locking the building.

1. Where did Din have a job?

_____

2. What was his job?

_____

3. What shift did he work?

_____

4. What was he in charge of doing?

_____

5. Who gave Din a raise?

_____

6. Who gave Din the keys to the building?

_____

7. Why did Din get a raise?

_____

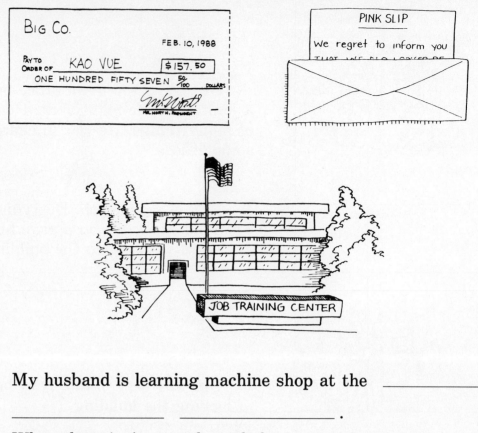

1. My husband is learning machine shop at the _____ _____ _____ .

2. When there isn't enough work for everyone, you get _____ _____ .

3. She works at night. She works the _____ _____ .

4. Jan works part-time. He's an _____ _____ .

5. Today is payday. I get my _____ .